GODDESS
POWER

GODDESS POWER

10 Empowering Tales of Legendary Women

YUNG IN CHAE

Illustrations by Alida Massari

ROCKRIDGE
PRESS

Illustration © 2019 Alida Massari
 Author photo courtesy of © Yung In Chae
Interior and Cover Designer: Regina Stadnik
Art Producer: Karen Williams
Editor: Mary Colgan
Production Editor: Jenna Dutton

ISBN: Print 978-1-64611-293-7 | eBook 978-1-64611-294-4

R0

For Donna, Sarah, and Tori
Goddesses in their own ways

CONTENTS

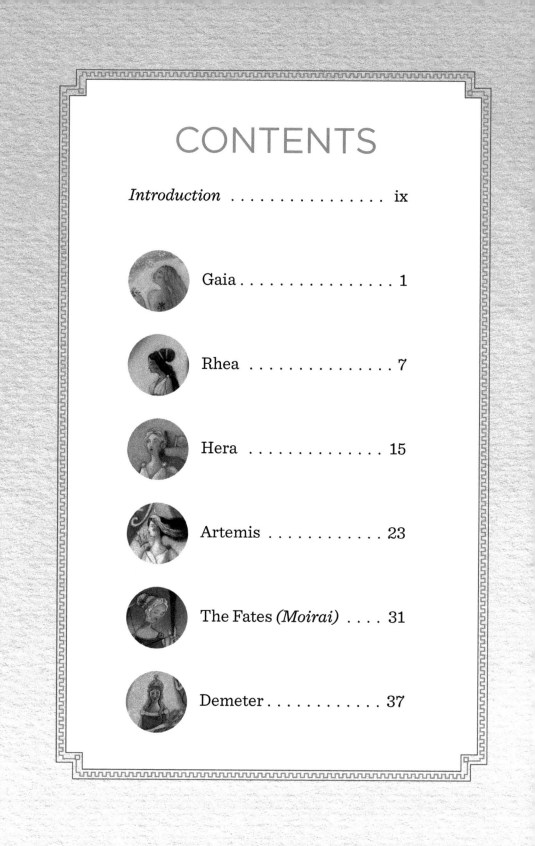

INTRODUCTION

Today, a myth is either a story or a falsehood. In the past, a myth was a story, but not necessarily a false story: more important than whether myths were fact or fiction was their *function*. Myths explain and entertain. They try to make sense of a nonsensical world. They impose a structure on it so that it becomes a little more knowable, a little less terrifying.

This book centers on goddesses in classical mythology. The word "classical" means a few different things; here it denotes the ancient Greeks and Romans, who shared many deities but called them by different names. (The queen of the gods was "Hera" to the Greeks but "Juno" to the Romans, for example.) I used the Greek names but drew upon sources from both cultures in order to paint you a richer portrait of each goddess.

Different cultures have different mythologies; classical mythology is just one example. Inevitably, it reflects the particulars of its time and place. But people from different times and places have found these myths compelling. Sometimes they relate to them profoundly. Other times, they revel in how unfamiliar this world is. Connections can happen in more than one way.

In contrast to some other deities, classical gods and goddesses take the form of human beings—and act like them. Notably, they are not infallible: Myths are as much about their blunders as about their triumphs. The similarities give people an opportunity for self-reflection. But because gods and goddesses are meant to be *more*—more than mortal, with more abilities—they let people think about what they could be as well as what they are.

Why limit the scope to goddesses, and thus limit the range of stories? While there are plenty of books about classical mythology in general, goddesses rarely get to monopolize the reader's attention. I wanted a space just for pondering female deities and, by extension, women and girls: all that we are, everything that we can do.

You will encounter ten myths in this book. Two feature ancestral goddesses, Gaia and Rhea. Five are about "Olympians," the gods and goddesses who live on Mount Olympus: Hera, Artemis, Demeter, Athena, and Aphrodite. The Fates and Muses are groups of goddesses with understated yet critical roles. Finally, Circe will take you on a long journey, one that hopefully leads to many others. The chapters follow a loose narrative sequence, but you may read them out of order if you like.

These goddesses have many admirable qualities. They are intelligent and resourceful. They are generous. They are protective of those they love. But they are far from flawless. They can also be petty and cruel. Often, they are unjust. (Beings who are above justice rarely want to show it to others.) They fail, repeatedly, to be kind to those who need kindness the most.

The thing to keep in mind is that goddesses are not meant to be flawless, any more than mortal women and girls are meant to be flawless. Nor are they meant to be role models, exactly. They simply exist, in all of their complexity—often, even that takes a lot of courage. What you take away from their accomplishments and mistakes is up to you. The stories offer possibilities, not instructions. And the possibilities are as varied as the goddesses themselves.

So take a seat and start reading. Listen to what the goddesses have to tell you. *Welcome, we've been waiting for you,* they'll say. They have been waiting for a long time.

GAIA

GUY-ah

GODDESS OF THE EARTH

FAMILY	Chaos (*father*)
	Uranus (*son and husband*)
	Various children
SYMBOLS	The Earth and all life on it
STRENGTHS	Creation

In the beginning, there was Chaos. Nothing else. Then out of that Chaos appeared a goddess named Gaia. Gaia was the goddess of the Earth, and she *was* the Earth. It was from her that anything with even a little bit of life came forth: plants and animals and mortals and deities. She was the true beginning of all things.

This meant that she was the ancestor of the Olympians—the twelve gods and goddesses who called snow-capped, cloud-wrapped Mount Olympus home. But before the Olympians ever ruled the sky and Earth and sea and Underworld, there were the primordial deities—the gods and goddesses who came immediately after Gaia. And this is where our stories begin.

The first thing to emerge after Gaia was not a deity. It was Tartarus, the gloomy dungeon so far below that it takes the same amount of time to get there from Earth as it does to get to the farthest reaches of sky. Then Eros (love) arrived to bring immeasurable joy and pain, followed by Erebus (darkness) and Nyx (the night). Nyx birthed Aether (light) and Hemera (the day).

As all of this was happening, Gaia got to work. She could achieve a lot very quickly, in part because she possessed the remarkable ability to have children without help. That's how she brought forth the Ourea (the mountains) and Pontus (the sea). But if she chose to, she could have a father for her children rather than have them by herself. Pontus fathered five of Gaia's children, who, like him, became sea gods and goddesses: Nereus, Thaumas, Phorcys, Ceto, and Eurybia.

Gaia would get a bit chilly at night, so next she created Uranus, who embodied the heavens brimming with stars, to cover her like a blanket. They married and had twelve children who were the original Titans, six girls and six boys. Their names were Oceanus, Coeus, Crius, Hyperion, Iapetus, Theia, Rhea, Themis, Mnemosyne, Phoebe,

Tethys, and—the youngest, with the temperament of a starved beast—Cronus.

But Gaia wanted still more children with Uranus. Next she gave birth to the three Cyclopes: Brontes, Steropes, and Arges. Although the Cyclopes were massive beings, what truly set them apart was the single eye blinking in the middle of their foreheads. They were skilled craftsmen and could create the most splendid tools and weapons.

Gaia then birthed three more children called Cottus, Briareos, and Gyges, together known as the Hecatonchires. They were strong, towering giants with fifty heads and a hundred arms each.

Gaia loved every one of her children, even more so because of their oddness. Uranus didn't feel the same way. He liked the Titans just fine, but he couldn't look at the Cyclopes and Hecatonchires without his stomach flying up to his throat. He hated the idea that he had fathered these creatures. He hated it almost as much as he hated the fact that Gaia didn't actually need him to father anyone. Eventually he decided that he wouldn't put up with his sons, reminders of his weakness, any longer.

While Gaia was elsewhere, Uranus locked up the Cyclopes and Hecatonchires in dark, damp Tartarus. But even without seeing the treacherous act, Gaia could hear her sons' wails ringing in her ears, feel them jumping and beating the walls of Tartarus in her chest. She rushed to Uranus and shouted at him to let them go. Then she tried to reason with him. Finally, she begged. But he steadfastly refused.

Gaia felt as though she were drying up and cracking open. Her heart hurt at the loss of her children. Her head hurt from witnessing the depths of her husband's cruelty. But when she reached into her grief she found, at the center, a solid, unyielding truth: She had to save her sons. And to do that, she had to get rid their father.

Her hunger for justice gave Gaia the strength to devise a plan. First, she made a large piece of flint and used it to fashion a sickle. Then she gathered her other children, the Titans, and announced that she had an important task for them.

"Your father has imprisoned your brothers, the glorious Cyclopes and Hecatonchires. He has trapped them deep in Tartarus, a place that no light touches and no sound reaches. My poor children, born from such a father, who among you wishes to right this wrong?" She held up the sickle. Its curved, jagged blade looked like a crescent moon with teeth.

Eleven of the Titans looked away, unsure if they dared harm their own father. But Cronus stepped forward, palm outstretched. "I'll do it, Mother. A father who would do such an evil deed is no father of mine," he said. Gaia smiled and handed him the sickle.

Gaia and Cronus returned home, whereupon Cronus hid nearby while Gaia prepared to pretend that she had swallowed her sadness. When Uranus approached, Gaia extended her arms, as if to embrace him. But the second he got close, open and vulnerable, Cronus jumped out from his hiding place and slashed his father with the sickle.

Blood poured from Uranus. Some of it fell on the Earth like drops of rain. Where the blood landed, new life sprouted like the first flowers of spring. From one spot burst forth the Erinyes, or Furies, goddesses of revenge who fly around torturing wrongdoers. Armor-clad Giants clambered out of another spot, followed by tree nymphs called the Meliae. A piece of Uranus's flesh tumbled into the sea and turned into an important goddess called Aphrodite.

As for Uranus, the last anyone saw of him was as he slunk away in shame, clutching at his wounds. After that, nobody ever heard from him again.

RHEA

RAY-ah

FAMILY	Gaia (*mother*) | Uranus (*father*)
	Cronus (*brother and husband*)
	Hestia (*daughter*)
	Demeter (*daughter*)
	Hera (*daughter*) | Hades (*son*)
	Poseidon (*son*) | Zeus (*son*)
SYMBOLS	Lion, tambourine
STRENGTH	Fertility

With Uranus gone, Cronus declared himself ruler of the universe. He married Rhea, one of his Titaness sisters. Everyone and everything submitted to his power. But Cronus couldn't shake the feeling that something bad was going to happen.

At night he often dreamed of his father, who would say just one thing over and over to him:

What you did to me, your child will do to you.

But Cronus wasn't the only one still suffering. Gaia had believed that Uranus's banishment was the key to her imprisoned sons' freedom. She was wrong: Cronus decided that he couldn't risk threats to his throne, so he refused to free the Cyclopes and Hecatonchires from Tartarus. Gaia left Cronus's side, disgusted that her son turned out to be no better than his father.

In time, Rhea had a child: a sweet-tempered goddess whom she named Hestia. As she watched Hestia take in the world for the first time, Rhea felt a powerful love burn in her chest. She handed the baby to Cronus so that he could share in her joy.

But when Cronus looked into Hestia's small and trusting face, all he could see was his father warning him that one of his children would overthrow him. Before Rhea knew what was happening, Cronus opened his mouth wide and swallowed Hestia whole.

Rhea cried and cried for her baby, but Cronus didn't care. He enjoyed having the power to make the entire world bend to his whim and will. He loved that power more than he would ever love any of his children.

Rhea's life became a blur of carrying and birthing babies only to have Cronus take them from her. She barely had time to marvel at how her next daughter, Demeter, was born with cascades of hair before the child disappeared into the dark hole of Cronus's mouth. She didn't even get to hold Hera, who looked as though she had been hammered out of gold, before Cronus snatched her away.

Her fourth child and first son, Hades, didn't stop screaming from the moment he was born to the moment when his father gulped him down. Rhea heard the echoes of his screams for several seconds after. By the time she had another son, Poseidon, Rhea's heart was so tattered that she couldn't look at him.

Rhea was a mother, many times over, who did not have a child. She was flooded with the instinct to protect her offspring yet drowning in the fact that she could not. What would they have been like? Would they have been kind? Mischievous? Clever? Heartless? Would they have gotten along with each other? Rhea had no way of knowing. She watched her siblings, the other Titans, play with their children, thinking about her own stuck in the pit of Cronus's belly. Rhea made a decision: She wouldn't have any more babies. She couldn't go through such heartbreak again. Then she found out that she was pregnant for the sixth time.

Once Rhea accepted this news, she made another decision—she was going to save this baby. But she couldn't do it alone. So she went to the only person she trusted: her mother. Gaia was more than happy to plot against Cronus after he had broken his promise to rescue her sons from Tartarus.

When Rhea was about to give birth, Gaia sent her away to an island called Crete. In a well-concealed cave on

Mount Ida, Rhea brought forth another boy, named Zeus. She tasked a group of her followers, the Kouretes, with noisily clanging their spears and shields at the mouth of the cave so that Cronus wouldn't hear the baby's cries. She also left a goat named Amalthea to nurse and raise Zeus in her stead. It hurt Rhea not to be with her baby, but she bore the pain because she knew that their separation was for his own good.

Rhea returned home, where Cronus was waiting. She held a rock that she had wrapped in swaddling clothes so that it resembled a newborn. While she pretended to nurse the rock, Cronus grabbed and swallowed it like he had the others. Then he wandered away, ignorant of the fact that his son was alive and safe on Crete, not wasting away in his stomach acid. When he was out of sight, Rhea sighed with relief.

Years passed. Rhea would periodically check in with Amalthea to see how Zeus was doing. Zeus soon grew up to be a healthy and handsome god. Once he was old enough, Gaia gave her grandson a special potion and told him to feed it to his father. This, she told him, was the key to rescuing his brothers and sisters from their father's swollen belly. Once they were out, she added, he had to go get his six uncles from Tartarus as well. Zeus agreed.

Zeus went to his parents' home, posing as a cupbearer with the innocent job of bringing nectar for Cronus to drink. Since father and son had never met, Zeus was able to slip Gaia's potion into a cup and hand it to Cronus without rousing his suspicion. As soon as Cronus drank from the cup, a violent storm stirred in his stomach, then thrashed upward until he could no longer hold it in.

First, he threw up a swaddled stone. Then, he threw up his children in reverse order of birth: Poseidon, Hades, Hera, Demeter, and Hestia. They had grown up inside Cronus and were now full-fledged gods and goddesses, so resplendent that it hurt to look at them.

They outnumbered Cronus. They could easily overpower him. Rather than fight a losing battle, Cronus abdicated his throne and ran away.

Zeus kept his promise to Gaia and released the Cyclopes and Hecatonchires. At long last, the unwanted sons of Uranus were free.

For a moment it seemed as though Rhea's children would divide up the universe and look after it together, with Zeus as king. But her Titan siblings had other ideas. They didn't want their young, inexperienced nephew to rule. They rose up against him. This resulted in a great war between the Titans and the new generation of gods.

But Zeus and his siblings had the grateful Cyclopes and Hecatonchires on their side. The Cyclopes made weapons for them with their great skills: Zeus received thunderbolts, Poseidon a trident, and Hades a cap of invisibility. The Hecatonchires threw rocks with their numerous hands. After ten long years of fighting, the Titans lost.

Zeus locked up most of the Titans in Tartarus, with the Hecatonchires standing guard. Atlas, the leader of the Titans, was sentenced to carry the world on his shoulders. Gaia was bitter that Zeus had freed her children only to imprison more of them. She birthed two monsters to avenge the Titans. One was Typhon, a giant with a hundred snake heads on his shoulders—possibly the most terrifying creature the world has ever seen. The other was his wife, Echidna, who was half woman and half snake.

Zeus vanquished Typhon by trapping him under Mount Etna, where even today he breathes fire in rage. But he let Echidna and her children go. Typhon and Echidna's offspring would later terrorize many heroes. One of them, a three-headed dog called Cerberus, guards the gates of the Underworld. Another, the Hydra, was a many-headed snake that breathed poison.

But for the most part, there was peace. Zeus claimed the heavens. Hera became his queen. Poseidon ruled the sea, Hades the Underworld. Demeter oversaw the harvest. Hestia sat down in front of her domain, the hearth.

Thus began the age of the Olympians, the gods and goddesses on Mount Olympus: grandchildren of Gaia, children of Rhea.

HERA

HEH-rah

GODDESS OF WOMEN, MARRIAGE,
CHILDBIRTH, AND FAMILY

FAMILY	Rhea (*mother*) | Cronus (*father*)
	Hestia (*sister*) | Demeter (*sister*)
	Hades (*brother*)
	Poseidon (*brother*)
	Zeus (*brother and husband*)
	Ares (*son*) | Eileithyia (*daughter*)
	Hebe (*daughter*) | Hephaestus (*son*)
SYMBOLS	Cow, diadem, lily, peacock,
	pomegranate, scepter
STRENGTHS	Fertility, vengeance

Hera was the queen of the gods. With her husband, Zeus, she had four children. One was Ares, the god of war. Another was Hephaestus, the blacksmith god.

Hebe, their daughter, was the Olympian cupbearer, in charge of pouring ambrosia and nectar for the gods and goddesses. Their other daughter, Eileithyia, was the goddess of midwifery.

Hera was the goddess of matters regarding the home. She blessed marriages, taking it upon herself to protect wives in particular. She presided over births, with Eileithyia assisting women in labor. She looked after families.

Despite her responsibilities, Hera's own marriage was not without its troubles. She and Zeus were often at odds with each other. Hera was a spirited, uncontrollable goddess. When she was happy, she was captivating. But when she was angry, she was the only thing in the universe that made Zeus quake with fear.

Most of the couple's problems were caused by Zeus's constant cheating. Hera was always catching her husband in the arms of other goddesses, nymphs, and mortal women. She was not one to sit by idly as he dishonored both her and the institution of marriage: When she learned about an affair, she let her molten wrath flow. And Zeus, for all of his power, was powerless to stop her. Hera never failed to get her revenge.

She learned early on in her marriage that it never hurt to be suspicious of Zeus. After a while, she even developed an unerring sense for when her husband was hiding or lying. Once, she looked down and spotted a cloud floating all alone, like a sheep that had separated from its flock. *That doesn't look right*, she thought. She went to investigate.

Hera was right: Zeus had made the cloud to cover himself and Io, a princess of Argos. When Zeus heard Hera approaching, he hastily transformed Io. Hera peeped through the fluffy wall and found her husband petting a gleaming cow.

She wasn't fooled; she knew her husband better than anyone. But looking into the cow's big, bottomless eyes—so much like her own—she got an idea. Hera put on an innocent smile and turned to Zeus.

"Oh! What a pretty little cow," she said sweetly. "Will you give it to me as a present?" Zeus couldn't think of a reason to say no, so he had to look on helplessly as Hera led Io away. Hera brought Io to Argus Panoptes, a giant with eyes embedded all over his body like stars in the sky. She told Argus, a loyal servant of hers, to guard the cow with his life.

Back on Mount Olympus, Zeus was distressed. He wanted to save Io, but he knew that he couldn't do it himself without starting a fight with Hera. He gave it some thought and sent his son Hermes, the messenger god, in his place.

Argus was an excellent guard. At least half of his eyes remained open at any given time, making it almost impossible to sneak past him unnoticed. Hermes had to be clever. When he got to the mountain where Argus had taken Io, he began playing a drowsy melody on his pipes. Hermes watched Argus's eyes close one by one. When the last eye was shut, he slew the giant and set Io free.

When Hera heard about Argus's death, she was devastated. To thank him for his service, she took his many eyes and placed them on the feathers of her favorite bird, the peacock, where they remain to this day.

Another time, Hera was searching for Zeus in the woods. She had caught a glimpse of her husband there, and she knew that he was off with some nymph. But where was he? Hera spotted a flash of light behind a grove. *Aha,* she thought, ready to pounce.

Suddenly, a nymph came into view and blocked Hera's path. "Greetings, Goddess. What brings you to our neck of the woods today? How lucky we are to host the great Hera, queen of the gods." And on and on she went, saying so much while saying nothing at all.

Hera impatiently shoved the nymph, whose name was Echo, aside. But it was too late; the light was gone. She ran toward the grove and found only matted grass among the trees. She knew that Zeus had been there. She realized something else: Echo had delayed her with chitchat so that Zeus and his lover could escape.

A nymph making a fool out of the queen of the gods— Hera was speechless with anger. Then her momentary inability to speak gave her an idea. She faced Echo. "You tricked me with your tongue," she said, "so your tongue will serve you no more."

Echo felt her throat constrict. She tried to beg for mercy, but all she could manage was to repeat Hera's final words: "No more." Satisfied, Hera flew away in her chariot drawn by peacocks.

Later, Echo fell in love with a handsome young man named Narcissus. But she couldn't tell him how she felt because she could only say his last words back to him. When she tried to fling her arms around his neck, he ran away. Echo was so heartbroken that her body crumbled into dust and blew away in the wind.

All that remained of her was her voice, which stayed in the mountains. We call that an *echo*, after the unfortunate nymph.

Hera's resentment reached new heights when Zeus brought home a baby boy born from his affair with a mortal woman named Alcmene. While Hera was asleep, Zeus suckled the baby at her breast so that he would grow strong. But the baby nursed so ferociously that Hera woke up. Furious, she pushed the infant away, spraying milk on the sky and creating the splatter of stars now known as the Milky Way.

Zeus named the child "Heracles," meaning "glory of Hera," in an attempt to soothe her anger. It didn't work. When Heracles was still a baby, Hera sent two snakes to kill him in his crib. But Heracles was already so strong that he strangled the snakes to death and played with them like toys.

When Heracles was a grown man, with a wife and two children, Hera made him go mad and kill them. As punishment for his family's murders, Heracles had to perform ten labors for King Eurystheus of Tiryns. He slew the Nemean Lion and the Hydra. He caught the Ceryneian Hind, a deer that was sacred to Artemis, as well as the Erymanthian Boar. He had to clean the Augean stables, which held three thousand cattle with poisonous feces, in a single day. He shot the man-eating Stymphalian Birds. He captured the Cretan Bull and stole the flesh-eating Mares of Diomedes. He convinced Hippolyta, the queen of the Amazons, to give him her girdle. Finally, he obtained the Cattle of Geryon, which were guarded by a two-headed dog, a herdsman, and a monster with three heads.

But King Eurystheus told Heracles that two of his labors didn't count because he had had help. So Heracles had to do two more, bringing the total number of labors to twelve. For the eleventh, he stole the golden apples of the Hesperides, the nymphs of the evening. The tree grew in Hera's orchard and she had tasked a hundred-headed dragon with guarding it. For the twelfth, Heracles went down to the Underworld and brought back Cerberus, the three-headed dog.

For completing the twelve labors, Heracles was made immortal. It was then that Hera put the past behind her and accepted him as a god. She let Heracles marry her daughter Hebe. Even Hera was impressed once in a while.

ARTEMIS

AHR-tuh-miss

GODDESS OF THE MOON,
HUNTING, WOODS, WILDLIFE,
AND MAIDENHOOD

FAMILY	Leto (*mother*) | Zeus (*father*)
	Apollo (*twin brother*)
	Various half-siblings
SYMBOLS	Bow and arrow, cypress,
	deer, moon
STRENGTHS	Hunting, midwifery

A very pregnant nymph named Leto collapsed on the ground. She could feel that she was close to giving birth, but she had nowhere to go and was exhausted from wandering.

The father of her baby was Zeus, the king of the gods. Zeus's wife, Hera, had gotten so angry when she found out about Leto's pregnancy that she banned any place on earth from providing her with shelter. Now Leto was on the move, unable to stop and unable to have her baby.

"Please let me stay here," Leto begged at every village, town, and city she came across. People would see her swollen stomach and feel pity rise in their hearts, but their fear of Hera's rage swiftly eclipsed any other feeling. In the end, the answer was always no.

Just as Leto was about to give up, she heard a voice calling her name. She turned around and saw the small island of Delos bobbing in the sea. "You have no home upon the Earth," the island told her, "and neither do I." Since Delos floated freely in the water, unanchored to firm land, Hera's ban didn't apply to it. Therefore, Leto was able to rest on the island until she gave birth—not to one child, but to two.

First, a girl with hair as black as midnight came into the world. Because she was a goddess, the girl could do many impressive things as soon as she was born. When she opened her eyes and saw her mother still in labor, she felt awful, almost as if she were experiencing the pain herself. *I can help with that*, she realized. So the first thing the girl did in life was bring forth her twin, a boy with hair as golden as midday. Leto named the boy Apollo, and the girl Artemis.

When Apollo grew up, he became the god of the sun. He had a bow and arrows forged from gold. Artemis became the goddess of the moon. Her bow and arrows were made of

silver, and she liked to use them to hunt. You could often
find her hunting in the woods, wearing a tunic that
skimmed her knees, with a pack of dogs by her side and a
team of deer pulling her chariot. Nobody, mortal or deity,
could hunt as well as Artemis, and she became the goddess
of hunting as well.

Artemis was an exceptional goddess, sure-footed and
sure of who she was. She knew that she wanted to remain
unmarried. Many women admired Artemis. They became
her followers, joining her on hunts and also vowing never
to marry.

Perhaps inspired by her role in Apollo's delivery,
Artemis took an interest in childbirth. She considered it
her duty to help women have babies as painlessly as pos-
sible. But Artemis could bring death as easily as she could
bring life. She was a goddess with a keen sense of justice:
She wanted to reward those who did right and punish those
who did wrong. And one mortal who did her wrong was a
young man named Actaeon.

Actaeon was hunting in the same woods at the same
time as Artemis, who was with her band of nymphs. After
many hours of chasing animals, the goddess decided that
the nymphs deserved a break. She led them to a grove,
in the middle of which sat a small grotto, so exquisite
that it looked as though it had been carved by a sculptor.
The grotto contained a pool with cold, glistening waters—
perfect for bathing after a long hunt.

Actaeon had lost his way and was wandering aimlessly
when he came across the grotto. He couldn't help but stop

and admire it. A place so magnificent on the outside surely had something even greater inside. He went in, only to find Artemis and her nymphs lounging in the waters, having completely shed their clothing.

Actaeon should have looked away. He should have turned around and left. Instead, he just stood there, staring at the goddess's beauty. The nymphs tried to cover Artemis's body with their own, but she towered above them.

Artemis felt herself redden to the temples, anger twisting like a hurricane inside her. She was angry not only because he had seen her, but also because he didn't seem to be sorry about it. She started to reach for her silver bow and arrow, then realized that she had leaned them against the side of the grotto. She thought fast and reached into the pool for a handful of water, which she flung at Actaeon's face. "Now go and tell everybody that you saw the goddess Artemis undressed—if you can!" she shouted.

As soon as the water hit him, Actaeon began to transform. He hunched over. His limbs grew long and skinny. Two ears sprouted from the top of his head. His pupils grew very large and very dark. By the end, he resembled nothing more than a deer.

Actaeon the deer stumbled out of the grotto and tried to make his way back home. While still in the grove, he encountered his hunting dogs, who no longer recognized him. Actaeon had heard those low growls enough times to know that he was in serious danger, and he ran as fast as his four spindly legs would allow. But before he could escape the woods, his hounds caught up and ate him.

Another mortal who got on Artemis's bad side was Niobe, the queen of Thebes. Every year, the Thebans held a celebration in honor of Leto and the miracle of her twins, Artemis and her brother Apollo. Niobe was extremely unhappy about this.

"Why worship Leto, who barely found a place to give birth and who has only two children, when you could worship me, the mother of fourteen: seven daughters and seven sons? Stop the festivities at once!" she ordered the Thebans, who had to obey their queen.

When Leto heard about Niobe's command, she was furious. She called Artemis and Apollo to her side and told them what happened.

"Are you going to allow Niobe to disrespect me, the proud mother of you two? Are you going to let the Thebans stop worshipping us as they should?"

"Of course not," the twins replied, promising their mother that they would make Niobe pay many times over. Artemis reached for her bow of silver, Apollo for his bow of gold, and they headed to Thebes together.

Niobe's seven sons were at home riding their horses. Suddenly, the eldest let out a sharp cry and fell to the ground, an arrow in his heart, his breath slowing to a still. From above, Apollo drew his bow again and proceeded to shoot six more times.

When Niobe rushed outside and saw her slain sons, she grew frantic with grief. But she refused to back down. "You may think you've won, Leto," she shouted at the sky. "But don't forget that I have seven children left—still five more than you!" She gestured at her seven daughters, who had come to mourn their brothers.

Artemis had not forgotten about Niobe's remaining seven children. She took aim and shot six of the girls one by one, from eldest to youngest. They fell quickly and quietly, as if on their own. Artemis was aiming at the last girl when Niobe embraced her daughter and asked for mercy.

"Please, she's all I have left!" Niobe cried. But Artemis, remembering her own mother's heartache and humiliation, shot a final arrow into the child.

Niobe looked around and saw all fourteen of her children dead. She fell to her knees. Her heart hardened until it turned into stone, then her entire body followed. But her tears kept flowing. Niobe became a statue that could not stop weeping for everything she had lost.

Artemis was strong and caring, loyal and protective: a great daughter, sister, and leader. But you never wanted to mess with her.

THE FATES
(MOIRAI)

MOY-rye

FAMILY   Each other (*sisters*)

SYMBOLS   Distaff, spindle, measuring rod, shears

STRENGTHS   Controlling lives

The fates of everybody in the world lay in the hands of three sisters. These goddesses were known, appropriately, as the Fates, or *Moirai.*

They worked alongside one another, dressed in flowing robes, and decided how every person lived, and for how long. Once the Fates made their choices, even the Olympians couldn't force them to choose otherwise. In a way, the Fates were more powerful than any of the deities.

The first sister was named Clotho. She wrapped the fibers of life around her spindle and spun them into thread. While doing so, she determined when a person was born and what peaks and valleys would dot the landscape of their lifetime.

The second sister was named Lachesis. Using a rod, she carefully measured the length of each thread that Clotho spun. Sometimes, Lachesis let a thread go on for yards and yards until it resembled an overgrown snake. Other times, she would stop a thread before it had truly begun, or right when it had started to take shape. There wasn't always logic or justice in Lachesis's decisions. She mostly based them on how she felt in the moment.

The third sister was named Atropos. She was actually the oldest sister, but her job required her to stand at the end of the little assembly line that they had set up for themselves. Atropos waited as Clotho spun the thread. She watched as Lachesis measured it with her rod. And then, when the moment and manner were right, she snipped it in two with her shears.

The Fates stayed out of sight for the most part, preferring to make things hum from behind the scenes. But on occasion they intervened . . . and made things much more interesting.

Once they intervened because a mortal was making it impossible for them to do their job. That mortal was Asclepius, the son of Apollo and the Thessalian princess Coronis. Asclepius was a gifted healer, to the point that he eventually learned how to bring people back from the dead. The Fates complained to Zeus that Asclepius was undoing their hard work. So Zeus killed Asclepius with a thunderbolt to satisfy the sisters.

When Apollo found out about his son's death, he was outraged. But what could he do? Zeus was his father. Instead, he slew the Cyclopes that made Zeus's thunderbolt.

As punishment, Zeus sent Apollo away from Olympus for a year to serve Admetus, the king of Pherae in Thessaly. Despite the circumstances, Admetus proved to be a kind host, and Apollo became his friend. After his exile ended, Apollo decided to thank Admetus by asking the Fates not to cut the king's thread when his time came. The Fates agreed—on the condition that someone else die in his place.

Admetus asked his servants, his soldiers, and even his elderly parents, but nobody was willing to sacrifice themselves. Finally, his wife Alcestis, the very reason he wanted to live longer, announced that she would die for him, and she did.

Admetus spent the days following Alcestis's death regretting the starless existence that he had to endure without her. But then the hero Heracles came to visit, and he was so moved by the story of Alcestis's love that he forced Hades, the king of the Underworld, to give her back to Admetus.

Another time the Fates intervened was at the birth of the Calydonian prince Meleager, the son of Oeneus and Althaea. His mother had barely taken him in her arms when the sisters appeared.

"What a lovely child," Clotho murmured.

"It's too bad that he won't live long," Lachesis sighed.

"Just until the fire consumes that log." Atropos pointed to one burning in the hearth.

Althaea screamed and immediately grabbed the log from the fire. She extinguished the clinging flames and hid the log in a box so that her son would live much, much longer than the Fates had prophesied.

Thanks to his mother's quick thinking, Meleager grew up to become a hero, famous for his bravery and strength. When Artemis sent down the Calydonian boar to punish Oeneus for not worshipping her properly, Meleager led the charge against the vicious, destructive animal. Although Meleager was the one who killed the boar, the first person to wound it was the swift huntress Atalanta, so he gave her the boar's hide. Meleager's uncles, the brothers of his mother, Althaea, had also been part of the hunt, and they were upset that a woman got to keep the trophy. They started to argue with their nephew about it, and soon the argument got so heated that Meleager ran his spear through both of them.

When Althaea heard about her brothers' deaths, she was devastated at the thought that her son could do such a terrible thing. Squinting through her tears, she retrieved a box from a high shelf. She opened it and, for a moment, stared at the log that she had rescued from the hearth and tucked away many years ago. Then she tossed the log into the fire.

As the flames started to eat away at the log, Meleager dropped to the ground. He felt as though an invisible knife were peeling off his skin. But all he could do was writhe in pain until the relief of death came.

The Fates were right after all. They always are.

DEMETER

duh-MEE-tur

GODDESS OF THE HARVEST

FAMILY | Rhea (*mother*) | Cronus (*father*)
Hestia (*sister*) | Hera (*sister*)
Hades (*brother*)
Poseidon (*brother*) | Zeus (*brother*)
Persephone (*daughter*)

SYMBOLS | Wheat, cornucopia, torch

STRENGTHS | Agriculture

The goddess of the harvest, Demeter, had hair as thick and rippled as grain fields when the wind runs through them. She kept the ground rich for planting, performed the magic of transforming small seeds into tall, swaying crops, and grew the food that fed hungry mortals.

She is an extremely important goddess because she protected people from starvation.

Demeter, with Zeus, had a daughter named Persephone. As a child, Persephone was like the warmth of the sun. The other Olympians couldn't help but smile down at her, and she always beamed back. Wherever Demeter went, Persephone toddled right behind. No mother has ever loved her daughter so much. Goddesses live forever, but Demeter felt that, for Persephone, she would give up her immortality and die without hesitation.

Persephone had an idyllic childhood on Mount Olympus. She grew up to be a lovely young goddess, as graceful as a single stalk of wheat. Demeter and Persephone were closer than ever. But now that she was older, Persephone liked to wander on her own sometimes. While her mother took care of the harvest, she often ran off to play with a few nymphs. But she never ventured very far. Demeter got nervous whenever Persephone was out of her sight for too long. In Demeter's eyes, Persephone was still the baby who sat and played on her lap during Olympian feasts.

One day, Persephone was picking flowers in a vibrant, sweeping meadow with her friends. She had tied up her skirt so that it made a pouch to hold her treasures. Once in a while, she took a flower from the pouch and tucked it into her braid. Soon her hair looked as lush as the meadow itself.

Persephone had just bent down to pick a fiery poppy when she noticed the petals quivering. She looked up and saw a gash appearing in the ground, as if someone had plunged a knife into its hard shell. The nymphs scrambled and shouted for help. But Persephone was too frightened to move—her feet seemed to have grown roots.

The gash opened up. Out flew an ebony chariot, drawn by horses with smoke for manes. Riding in the chariot was Hades, the god of death and ruler of the Underworld. Persephone had seen her uncle a few times when she was younger, but it had been years since their last meeting. She barely recognized him. But Hades apparently recognized *her* as he charged toward where she was rooted.

Before Persephone could make a sound, Hades grabbed her around the waist and hoisted her onto his chariot, tearing her dress in the process. The flowers that she had so carefully gathered in the folds of her skirt fell on the grass in a soft, colorful shower. She tried to wriggle free, but Hades held her tight. The most she could do was push away his face with her palm. That didn't hurt him in the slightest—he just laughed. Tears dotted her cheeks, but that only made him laugh more. He was still laughing as the gash swallowed them both and healed itself.

Then everything was calm.

When Persephone didn't come home after the sun god Helios had finished making his rounds for the day, Demeter started to worry.

When Persephone was still absent well into the moon goddess Selene's flight, Demeter became desperate. She couldn't sleep. She walked the entire expanse of the Earth, asking every mortal and nymph and deity she found:

"Have you seen my daughter?"

"Do you know where Persephone is?"

The moon made room for the sun. The sun cleared the way for the moon. They circled the world again and again. But there was still no sign of Persephone. Then, Demeter happened upon the meadow where Persephone had been stolen by Hades. There she found, lying on a carpet of bruised flowers, the belt torn from Persephone's dress. Demeter held the belt in her hands, her mind refusing to accept the conclusion it offered. But she couldn't deny the truth. She now knew that someone had taken her daughter.

Her sorrow bled into the Earth. She didn't know who had kidnapped Persephone or where they had taken her. She had no leads. With the goddess of the harvest so depressed, all vegetation suffered. Crops began to wither and die along with her spirits. People had nothing to eat. They made sacrifices to Zeus, praying for him to intervene. But not even Zeus could convince Demeter to work when she was in such great pain.

Many days into her mourning, Demeter was sitting alone, lost in thought, when she heard the sea calling her name. A nymph named Arethusa poked her head out of the water. "Great Goddess, I can put an end to your search," she said. "I was swimming beneath the Earth, in the River Styx, when I passed by the Underworld and saw your Persephone: the reluctant queen of Hades." Then she slipped back into the waves.

First, Demeter felt nothing, so great was the shock. Then came a fury that made the inside of her head cloudy and hot. Once she composed herself, she headed straight for Mount Olympus to find Zeus.

Zeus was overjoyed to see Demeter, thinking that she had come to announce the end of the famine. Instead, she marched up to his throne and said, "Hades is the one who took Persephone. Make him give her back. I don't even care about punishing him for the crime. If you won't do it for me, do it for her—my daughter."

"*Our* daughter," Zeus corrected, and Demeter let herself believe, for a moment, that he cared about Persephone after all, and that everything was going to be all right. But the king of the gods pricked and deflated Demeter's swell of hope with his next words:

"You're angry. I understand why you're angry. And I promise I will take care of this. But you must not let your anger prevent you from being fair. Hades—our brother—did not commit a crime. It was an act of love, however misguided."

Zeus's words drenched Demeter like an icy waterfall. She nearly lunged at his throat, but stopped herself just in time, remembering, with bitterness, that she still needed his help.

"Just get my daughter home," she managed at last.

"Persephone will return to you," Zeus said, "as long as she has not touched any food from the Underworld. That is the Fates' rule, not mine."

Demeter looked him in the eye. "She hasn't eaten anything. She's too sad because of this monstrous *crime* that *your brother* committed."

Demeter was right: Persephone had not eaten a thing. In the beginning, as Demeter had guessed, Persephone's despair had driven away her appetite. Eventually, the pangs of hunger broke through her haze of sadness, and her refusal to eat became not a function of unhappiness but an act of resistance.

Persephone knew that she did not belong in the Underworld. She sensed that she could not take anything from it without paying a price.

Hades didn't know what to do. He offered Persephone delicious meats and sweets on ornate platters with vines decorating the edges to make the food more appealing. He asked his gardener, Ascalaphus, to grow new fruits and vegetables that she might like to try. None of it made a difference. Persephone continued to starve.

Once, Hades watched as Persephone picked up the figs that he had given her and threw them one by one against the wall, where they left a dark stain. He decided to have another chat with Ascalaphus.

Persephone watched the last fig splatter on the wall. She was determined not to accept anything Hades offered her. But with every passing day, resistance got a little harder. She had no energy. Even though she was always tired, she couldn't sleep for more than an hour at a time. She began to lose awareness of when she was awake and when she was asleep.

On a rare night when Persephone was able to sleep for a few hours, she dreamed that she had wandered into the gardens of the Underworld, which Ascalaphus had kindly showed her a couple of days before. In her dreams, the gardens were both more horrifying and more magnificent than they were in reality. From far away, everything looked dead, but up close, she could see that the gardens were bursting with life: There were plants that she knew and loved, and plants that she never could have imagined. She walked around until she spotted a pale red fruit hanging from a thin, crooked branch. A pomegranate.

She cracked it open and peered at the seeds nestled inside, glittering like jewels. Then, almost without thinking, she reached into the pomegranate's flesh, dug out a few seeds, and ate them. Those tiny, tart pearls were the most delicious things she had tasted in her life. She could feel each one burst on her tongue and fill her mouth with flavor.

Just as she was about to devour the entire fruit, a sharp voice—a lot like her mother's—called her name, cutting through the dark. The gardens shattered and faded.

Persephone woke up. She was hungrier than ever but hardly felt it, as she was so relieved that the pomegranate had been part of her dream. The voice calling her name was real, though. She could hear it, insistent, persistent, echoing from the main chambers.

She got dressed and went to Hades's throne room, where she saw Demeter pacing in the center, demanding to see Persephone, with Zeus and Hades standing to the side.

"Persephone! Where is my daughter? Persephone—I've come to get you!"

"Mother!" Persephone cried and ran toward Demeter's open arms. For a fleeting instant, mother and daughter were reunited within a bubble of infinite happiness.

Past her mother's shoulder, Persephone could see Ascalaphus approaching Hades and whispering in his ear. In one hand, he held a split pomegranate with several missing seeds. Persephone's gaze darted from the fruit to the grin spreading on Hades's face to her own fingers, intertwined with her mother's, streaked with a reddish juice.

She screamed. Her screams turned into sobs. Demeter pulled her daughter closer, begging to know what was wrong. Hades was talking to Zeus, pointing to the pomegranate. Zeus's face turned ashen. Hades laughed as he had laughed when he plucked Persephone from the meadow and dragged her into gloom. Demeter heard the laughter and turned toward her brothers. She, too, saw the pomegranate. She rushed over. She started yelling. Hades just kept laughing. Persephone tried to claim that she hadn't eaten the seeds. Then she admitted that she had and pleaded with her uncle to let this go; to let *her* go.

In the realm of death, there is deception and secrecy, but there is no denying the truth when it presents itself.

When everyone had calmed down, Zeus helped Demeter and Hades come to a compromise. Even Zeus could not go against the will of the Fates: Since Persephone had eaten the food of the Underworld, she would not be able to leave for good. But he did get all parties to agree to Persephone spending half of the year on Mount Olympus with Demeter, as her daughter, and half of the year in the Underworld with Hades, as his wife.

But wherever she was, whomever she was with, Persephone would first and foremost be herself. Her time as prisoner had taught her that she was far stronger than she had thought, a goddess capable of much grit and fight.

And so, Persephone accepted her fate. Six months out of the year, she rules the souls of the dead alongside Hades, with a tense jaw and a bloodless expression. But when she emerges from the Underworld for the other six months, a rosiness immediately blooms on her pale skin. Her eyes brighten, her curls regain their shine. Demeter has made the Earth especially bountiful to celebrate Persephone's return. Mother and daughter embrace. The world, despite all of its hidden darkness, becomes radiant again.

ATHENA

uh-THEE-na

GODDESS OF WISDOM AND WAR

FAMILY   Metis (*mother*)
Zeus (*father*)
Various half-siblings

SYMBOLS   Olive tree, owl, spear and shield

STRENGTHS   Wisdom, warfare

Zeus had a problem. Life had been going well for him up to this point. He had overthrown his father, Cronus, to become king of the gods. He was seeing a woman named Metis, a wise and beautiful Titaness. They were going to have a baby.

Then Zeus heard a prophecy that, if Metis had a son, he would overthrow Zeus like Zeus had overthrown Cronus. And Zeus wasn't ready to give up his throne.

After much pacing back and forth, he made a decision. He went to Metis and told her that he wanted to play a game. "Let's see who can become the smallest animal," he said. Metis agreed and turned herself into a shrinking menagerie of creatures: a fox, a bird, a mouse. When she became a fly, Zeus took the form of a frog and swallowed her.

Months later, Zeus got a splitting headache while at home on Mount Olympus. He felt like his head was actually going to split in half. When he couldn't take it anymore, he summoned his son Hephaestus, the blacksmith god, and asked him to break open his skull in hopes of relieving the pain.

Hephaestus swung his axe and brought it down on his father's head, making a sound like rocks bashing against each other. Dark, sweeping clouds moved into view, threads of lightning blinked, and thunder groaned in the distance. A shadowy figure sprang from the wound splitting Zeus's skull. Hephaestus dropped his axe and stepped back to stare with the other Olympians.

Once the sky brightened again, they could see that the figure was not a baby girl or boy, but a woman. She wore a full suit of armor and had eyes as gray and dramatic as the storm that had just passed. In one hand she held a spear; in the other a shield. Her mother, Metis, had crafted all of this from the inside of Zeus's head. This was Athena, no ordinary goddess, born of no ordinary birth.

From the moment of her emergence, Athena was fully formed, perfect: She didn't need to grow up the way that others do, because she was already who she was meant to be. She never wanted to marry; she had so much to accomplish. Naturally, the goddess who was born holding weaponry oversaw matters of war. Athena also became the goddess of wisdom, often accompanied by an owl. And she was indeed very wise.

One day, Athena spotted a hilly city from where she stood on Mount Olympus. It was attractive and vibrant, but also had character, and she immediately knew that she wanted it for herself. Without delay, she went down there from the mountain to stake her claim.

Seconds after she arrived, she heard a loud noise behind her. She turned around to see the ocean god Poseidon clutching his enormous trident, kelp tangled in his long, damp hair.

"Hello, Uncle Poseidon," Athena said, taken aback. "What are you doing here?"

"I'm taking this city," Poseidon replied, a bit startled himself. "What are *you* doing here?" And that's when they realized that they had come for the same reason.

"I should get this city," Athena argued. "I saw it first; I arrived before you did. And I could do more for its people than you ever could."

"No, *I* should get this city," Poseidon countered. "I am one of the oldest Olympians, the brother of Zeus, the mighty ruler of the vast oceans and everything in them. If I say that I want something, then it is mine."

They continued to argue until it became clear that they would never come to an agreement. They decided to settle the matter with a contest and summoned the king of the city to act as judge. The rules of the contest were simple: Whoever came up with the most useful gift for the city would win.

Poseidon went first. He slammed the base of his trident on the ground. Cracks formed where the trident struck, then widened until a jet of water burst forth and reached toward the sky. As the spurt of water lost its strength, it sank to the ground and pooled into a saltwater spring.

Then it was Athena's turn. Poseidon was a powerful god, as he had pointed out. He was also her uncle. Still, Athena refused to let him intimidate her. She gently tapped one of the cracks left by the trident with her spear. A sprout poked its head out of the dirt and quickly started to grow, as if an invisible force were tugging on it from above. Moments later, a majestic olive tree stood before them, looking as though it had been there forever.

It wasn't much of a competition. Poseidon's spring was filled with water too salty to drink. Athena's tree was far more useful. People could eat the olives or press them to make oil. They could even use the wood from the trunk. The king of the city declared Athena the winner. She became the patron goddess and protectress of the city, which named itself "Athens" after her. Athens went on to become a big and important place, home to a lot of political and cultural developments. Today, it is the capital of Greece.

Athens was a credit to Athena, who had always been an extremely proud goddess. The flip side of Athena's great pride, however, was that she easily bristled at insult. The most famous mortal to insult her was a Lydian girl named Arachne.

Arachne didn't come from wealth or a famous family, but she had something that neither could guarantee: true, pure talent. In Arachne's case, it was a talent for weaving. With just a few tools and some wool she would create staggering artwork. Her sharp, vibrant images seemed to be moving on the fabric or about to leap off it.

Watching Arachne weave was like watching a performance at the theater: The movements themselves were works of art. Nymphs and mortals alike came from all over to see her fingers dancing across the fabric, to listen to the music of the loom clicking, and to watch the drama of threads stitching together to form a story. For Arachne had learned to weave from the best: Athena herself.

Before long Arachne became convinced that *she* was the best, better than anyone, better even than Athena. The student had become the master. At first, Arachne kept the prideful thought to herself. Then she began to brag, telling a few of the people who came to watch her that if she were given the chance, she could beat Athena in a contest. Pretty soon, the entire city was buzzing about the girl whose weaving upstaged a goddess's.

The buzz traveled outward and upward, until it reached Mount Olympus and lodged itself in Athena's ear, irritating her day and night. Finally, she felt that she had no choice but to confront Arachne.

When Athena arrived in Lydia, Arachne was at her loom, surrounded by a group that watched her in reverent silence, as though observing a sacred ritual. Athena grew more annoyed than ever. She decided to set a trap. She swept streaks of gray into her hair, carved wrinkles into her forehead, and made herself wobbly and small. When she was finished, nobody could have guessed that she was a goddess and not an old woman.

Athena worked her way through the crowd until she was standing right next to Arachne. She tapped the girl on the shoulder.

"Listen to the advice of an old woman, for there is wisdom in age," Athena told Arachne. "You may call your-self the best weaver among mortals, but you must not claim to be superior to a goddess. Apologize to Athena right now and I am sure she will forgive you."

Arachne wrinkled her nose. "Thank you very much, but I didn't ask for your advice. And if it's so wrong to point out that I'm a better weaver than Athena, then why hasn't she shown up to answer my challenge?"

Athena revealed herself. "She has."

A gasp rippled through the crowd. Arachne clenched her jaw and fists, trying not to show how terrified she was. Much like Athena, Arachne was too proud to retreat once she had taken a stand. So the two of them sat down at their looms, each determined to create something that would surpass the other's.

Athena had a flair for the theatrical. She loved showing off in front of an audience, and competition made her skin crackle with electricity. She was looking forward to putting Arachne in her place.

The two competitors completed their weaving quickly and everyone gathered around to see the results. Athena's work was flawless. Her stitches were so clean that the images looked like drawings. The tapestry depicted her family performing all sorts of spectacular feats, and Athena couldn't resist adding scenes of them punishing mortal arrogance in the corners. She had topped it off with a border of olive leaves.

The audience sighed in admiration of Athena's tapestry. Then they turned to look at what Arachne had done.

On a technical level, Arachne's tapestry was also flaw-less. It was possibly the greatest one she had ever made. But the content made Athena widen her gray eyes, a deadly combination of envy and anger brewing within. In one scene, Zeus was seducing Europa by pretending to be a snowy bull. In another, Poseidon was turning into a bird to deceive Medusa. In yet another, Athena's half-brothers Apollo and Dionysus were also dressing up to trick women.

Athena was not afraid of the other Olympians. She had entered life by opening her father's head like a door. She had bested her uncle in a public contest. But gazing upon Arachne's tapestry, she realized that she needed mortals to fear the gods even if she didn't. She could not allow Arachne to get away with mocking her family.

Athena picked up her spear and sliced Arachne's tapestry into ragged strips. Then she lifted the wooden tool she used to hold her wool and began to whack Arachne on the head.

Humiliated, Arachne hanged herself on a nearby tree. It was only then that Athena felt pity for the poor girl whose extraordinary talent, the only thing of value that she owned, had led to her end. So she walked over to Arachne and touched her with a special herb.

The rope from which Arachne hung turned into a fine line of silk. The girl's body shrank and her arms and legs doubled in number. Arachne was now a spider, allowed to continue beyond death the work that she was born to do.

And this is why spiders belong to a group of animals called *arachnids*.

THE MUSES

MYOO-zuhz

GODDESSES OF INSPIRATION

FAMILY   Mnemosyne (*mother*)

Zeus (*father*)

Each other (*sisters*)

Various half-siblings

SYMBOLS   Writing tablet, stylus, scroll, books, instruments, masks, veil, globe, compass

STRENGTH   The arts

Once in a while, artists sit down to draw a picture, compose a song, write a poem—but nothing happens. The inspiration just won't flow, like a clogged fountain. In these situations, they have to call upon the Muses.

The Muses were the nine daughters of Mnemosyne, the goddess of memory, who was the Titaness daughter of Gaia and Uranus. Once, during a period of melancholy, Mnemosyne spent nine nights with Zeus. Nine months later, she gave birth to nine children:

- *Calliope*, the leader, was the Muse of epic poetry. She held a writing tablet and stylus pen.
- *Clio* was the Muse of history. She kept a scroll and a pile of books with her at all times.
- *Erato* was the Muse of lyric poetry, in particular love poetry. She held a stringed musical instrument called a cithara, which is a type of lyre.
- *Euterpe* was the Muse of music. She often played the aulos, a Greek flute.
- *Melpomene* was the Muse of tragedy. She carried a tragic mask, the kind that people wore on stage for performances of tragedies.
- *Polyhymnia* was the Muse of hymns. She wore a veil and was extremely serious, always pondering one issue or another.
- *Terpsichore* was the Muse of dance. She loved to dance while playing the lyre, a laurel wreath nestled in her hair.
- *Thalia*, the Muse of comedy, had a comedic mask. She was joyous and excelled at making people laugh.
- *Urania* was the Muse of astronomy. She used a globe and compass to look at the stars and interpret their positions.

No one was better than the Muses at their various arts. But that didn't stop some people from trying to outdo them anyway.

One day, Athena decided to pay a visit to the Muses, her half-sisters, in their valley on Mount Helicon: a stunning dimple of trees and caves and flowers. There was also a spring, Hippocrene, that the winged horse Pegasus had created by sinking his hoof into the ground. The beauty of Mount Helicon was inspiring enough, but the waters of Hippocrene actually had the power to give inspiration to poets who drank from it.

Here, in this pretty pocket, Athena found all of the Muses sitting together. She stopped to admire their home and especially Hippocrene, which she had never seen. Urania rose when she saw Athena approach and pulled her into a hug.

"I love the new spring," Athena said when Urania let her go. "I heard Pegasus made it—is that true? You're very fortunate to live in such a place."

"Yes, our home is wonderful. But nowhere is safe these days," Polyhymnia said solemnly. "We're still recovering from the time we were passing through the lands of King Pyreneus and he tried to trap us in his house."

"And don't forget the Pierides," Clio jumped in.

Athena was curious. "The Pierides?"

So Urania told Athena the story of the king and princesses who were foolish enough to take on the Muses.

Pierus was the king of Emathia in Macedon. He had nine daughters—the same number as the Muses, the king noted to himself. This fact stuck in his mind and grew like a well-watered weed until, to Pierus, it was more than coincidence: It was destiny. It was his daughters' destiny, he concluded, to triumph over the Muses.

Pierus's daughters, the Pierides, happened to possess delightful voices. Their father would often say that the nine of them together looked exactly like the nine Muses, and their singing was far superior. The Pierides didn't need much convincing before they believed it themselves. Before long, they were marching into Mount Helicon and challenging the Muses to a contest.

The Muses were embarrassed by the idea of competing with these girls. But it would be even more embarrassing to refuse the challenge. So the Pierides and the Muses agreed that each team would select a champion to perform a song on their behalf, with a panel of nymphs as judges.

The Pierides' champion sang a song about the great battle between the gods and the Giants for control of the cosmos. But in her version, the Giants were fearsome and awe-inspiring, while the gods were so cowardly that they fled and hid in the form of animals: Zeus became a ram, Hera a cow, and Aphrodite a fish.

Athena scowled as she listened to this part of Urania's story.

The Muses chose Calliope as their champion. She tied up her hair with a strand of ivy so that it wouldn't fall into her face and began singing the tale of Demeter and Persephone. Calliope's honeyed notes carried the nymphs through a whirlwind of emotions. They wept with Demeter when Hades abducted Persephone. They cheered when mother and daughter were reunited. They cried again when Zeus decided to make Persephone spend half of the year with Hades. As the Muse finished her song, the audience was quiet with rapture, hardly able to breathe.

It was never really a question. The nymphs unanimously chose the Muses as the winners.

But the Pierides did not accept defeat with grace. They stomped their feet, trampling the delicate grass. They shook their fists and hurled venomous insults at the Muses.

"Surely you punished the girls for such behavior?" an indignant Athena asked when Urania finished her story. As soon as the words left her mouth, a harsh greeting echoed through the woods. Athena was startled, but Urania just laughed and looked up at the branch stretching over their heads.

On it sat nine magpies, their feathers dull and scruffy, their eyes sparkling with mischief. The birds craned their necks and peered at the goddesses. They opened their beaks. They seemed to be trying to sing, but the only sound that they could choke out was idle chatter. And Athena knew just what had happened to the Pierides.

APHRODITE

aah-fro-DIE-tee

GODDESS OF LOVE AND BEAUTY

FAMILY   Uranus (*father*)
Hephaestus (*husband*)
Eros (*son*) | Aeneas (*son*)

SYMBOLS   Apple, dove, dolphin, mirror,
scallop shell

STRENGTHS   Affairs of the heart

When Cronus slashed his father, Uranus, with his sickle and Uranus fell to the Earth in pieces, a part of him fell into the sea as well. It hit the water near a place called Paphos, on Cyprus, and a bed of pale foam formed where it landed. From that foam rose a goddess, already an adult, covering herself with her long, wavy hair.

This was Aphrodite, goddess of love and beauty. She had no mother, no childhood, no past. Everything about her lay ahead.

Aphrodite stepped ashore and headed for Mount Olympus. The Olympians welcomed her as one of their own. They were at once awed by and wary of her beauty. All of the goddesses were beautiful beyond belief, and Aphrodite was not necessarily the most beautiful of all. But she had something—something difficult to describe yet impossible to deny. When she moved, the air around her seemed to slow. When she walked into a room, everything in it leaned forward. When you looked at her, you couldn't look away. You didn't want to look away. The image of her appeared sharper than everyone else's.

The moment that Zeus laid eyes on Aphrodite, he was overwhelmed with visions of conflict roiling among the gods. They would fight for her affections. There would be chaos. War, perhaps. No, he couldn't let that happen.

Zeus's solution was to offer Aphrodite his son Hephaestus for her husband. She wasn't thrilled about the match. Hephaestus, the blacksmith god, was reliable and hardworking. But he was also ugly—so much so that, when he was born, Hera, his own mother, hurled him off of Mount Olympus. The fall left him with a twisted foot. Nevertheless, Aphrodite dared not insult the king and the queen of the gods by refusing their son.

So Aphrodite and Hephaestus married. Hephaestus, for one, couldn't believe his luck. He lavished his wife with elaborate presents that he created himself: jewelry like fruits on the vine, and, unwisely, a girdle that rendered Aphrodite irresistible to almost everyone. But the gifts didn't make a difference in Aphrodite's heart. She looked at her marriage and could not see herself in it. She started looking for herself in other gods and mortal men.

Hephaestus had a brother named Ares, the god of war. In sharp contrast to Hephaestus, Ares was handsome, reckless, and unpredictable. Aphrodite was drawn to him, perhaps more so because he was so different from her husband. They soon became lovers. While Hephaestus was at his workshop, Aphrodite would bring Ares into their bed.

Neither took great pains to hide the affair. One day, the sun god Helios was riding his chariot across the sky when he spotted Aphrodite and Ares locked in an embrace. Helios rushed to Hephaestus and told him what he had seen.

Hephaestus was heartbroken. But he knew that if he tried to confront Aphrodite without proof, she would deny everything. He needed to catch her in the act. He used his tools to construct a net with fibers so fine that they were almost invisible and so strong that nothing could escape. He cast the net over the bed he shared with Aphrodite and waited.

As soon as Aphrodite and Ares tumbled onto the sheets, the net caught them like a pair of fish. They were stuck. Hephaestus thought that trapping them would make him feel better, but it only made him feel worse. Out of spite, he called upon the rest of the Olympians to come see the embarrassed lovers tangled up in each other.

Another of Aphrodite's love affairs came about because of her son, Eros, who some say was born out of Chaos but others say was fathered by Ares. According to the stories, Eros was a mischievous child, the little god of desire. He was armed with a bow and a quiver full of arrows. Eros could make anyone fall in love by shooting them with his arrows—even his mother. This became clear when, while leaning over to give Aphrodite a kiss, he accidentally poked her with an arrow.

Although Aphrodite was annoyed by her son's clumsiness, she didn't think much of the small scrape on her shoulder. She sent Eros away to play on his own and went for a walk. In a nearby forest, she happened upon Adonis, a young man born from the bulging bark of a myrrh tree. She instantly fell in love with his budding loveliness.

From then on, Aphrodite and Adonis were constantly together. Aphrodite preferred to nurture her beauty indoors, but when she learned that Adonis loved to hunt, she knotted her dress to keep it from dragging in the dirt and ran alongside him in rocky terrains. Still, she couldn't help but worry whenever he was alone in the woods or up in the mountains. She recalled stories about wild beasts boring holes in mortals, whose lives were as fragile as butterfly wings. She warned him to stay away from boars, wolves, bears, and lions, and to chase after rabbits and deer instead.

"Your beauty," she told him, "while of the greatest value to me, is no protection against fangs and claws."

But Adonis, being a careless youth, was only half-listening to his beloved's concerns. As soon as Aphrodite flew away in her sparrow-drawn chariot, he picked up his spear and returned to hunting. He heard his hounds bark, telling him that they had tracked down a boar. Adonis rushed over and threw his spear, but barely managed to scratch its hide.

The boar, now injured and angered, charged straight at Adonis and ran its tusks through his flesh, tearing through him as easily as if he were made out of paper. Then it kept running, deep into the trees, while Adonis bled on the grass.

Aphrodite heard Adonis's shouts of agony and turned her chariot around. When she got to him, the life had already evaporated from his eyes. Aphrodite held her dead lover in her lap and sobbed. She knew that she could not reverse the Fates' decision. But as a small gesture, she poured nectar over Adonis's blood, where it had soaked into the dirt, and a flower of the same striking red popped up. This is the delicate anemone, named for the winds that blow its petals away.

Aphrodite didn't just engage in love affairs, however. She once played a crucial role in an incident that changed the course of history. It started with a nymph surfacing from the sea as Aphrodite had long ago. The nymph, Thetis, was luminous like the moon. Her hair was still heavy with saltwater when Zeus and Poseidon began fighting for her attention. But the Fates put a swift end to their shoving match with a prophecy: Thetis's son, they said, would grow up to be greater than his father.

Poseidon felt as though he had been plunged into the iciest part of his ocean. Memories of Cronus's defeat flickered before Zeus's eyes. Wordlessly, the brothers came to the same conclusion: Thetis wasn't worth endangering their thrones.

Once again, Zeus decided that marriage was the solution. He arranged for Thetis to marry Peleus, the king of Phthia. As usual, the Fates turned out to be correct about Thetis: She would become the mother of Achilles, an epic warrior and the best of the Greeks, certainly greater than his father. But before Achilles was born, there was Thetis and Peleus's wedding.

The wedding was set to be an extravagant event. Any deity worth their altar was invited, except one: Eris, the goddess of discord. Nobody wanted to invite discord into the beginning of a marriage. But of course, Eris heard about a wedding that everybody else was attending. And she was not happy about the snub.

Eris was smart. She knew that there was no point in challenging the Olympians directly; she would definitely lose. The best revenge was sowing discord among them. She slipped unnoticed into the party. Hera, Aphrodite, and Athena were mingling in a corner. Eris waited until the three goddesses formed a triangle, then retrieved a golden apple from her sleeve and tossed it into their midst before disappearing.

Hera felt something knock against her heel. She turned around and picked up the golden apple. An inscription

caught her eye: *to the most beautiful*. Hera was pleased. "To the most beautiful," she read aloud. "That can only be me."

Aphrodite snatched the apple from Hera. "Someone clearly meant to give this to me."

"Be reasonable," Athena interjected. "The golden apple is mine."

The three goddesses asked Zeus to settle the matter. Zeus considered the candidates: his wife, his daughter-in-law, his daughter. He couldn't do it. He frantically looked around for an escape. His gaze landed on a handsome shepherd tending to his flock.

"There," Zeus said, pointing to the shepherd. "That man will choose for me."

Hera, Aphrodite, and Athena went to find the shepherd, whose name was Paris. He was startled by the goddesses' arrival, then again by their divine beauty. Paris stared at the apple that Hera had placed in his hand, genuinely unsure of what to do. How could he decide among these goddesses, all of whom were more beautiful than anyone he had ever seen?

"Give me the golden apple," Hera said at last, "and I will make you the most powerful man in the world."

"I will make you the wisest man in the world," Athena said.

"And I," Aphrodite said, "will make the most beautiful woman in the world your wife."

Paris, after the briefest of hesitations, knelt before Aphrodite and offered her the golden apple. She smiled and accepted the fruit while Hera and Athena smoked with anger.

It was a decision that led to a historic war. Paris, who turned out to be a long-lost prince of Troy, met the most beautiful woman in the world while on a diplomatic voyage: Helen, the queen of Sparta, and wife of Menelaus. Aphrodite was present when Paris and Helen met, eager to keep her promise. She told Eros, who had followed his mother, to shoot Helen with one of his arrows. In the middle of the night, Paris and Helen, newly in love, left for Troy together.

Menelaus was enraged when he learned that Paris had eloped with his wife. He went to his brother, Agamemnon, the king of Mycenae, who gathered forces from all over Greece to attack Troy, one of the most powerful cities in the world. The war lasted ten years. For a long time, there was no end to the fighting in sight. Then Odysseus, the king of Ithaca, came up with the idea of tricking the Trojans into accepting a wooden horse as a gift. Greek soldiers were hiding in the Trojan Horse. Once they were inside the city walls, the Greeks climbed out of the horse and killed every Trojan they could find.

The war ended with the total destruction of Troy. Nearly every member of the royal family was killed, with one notable exception: Aeneas, a son of Aphrodite by the Trojan prince Anchises. Aeneas rounded up the survivors and headed for what is now Italy, thus fulfilling his destiny: to set the stage for the founding of Rome.

CIRCE

SER-see

GODDESS OF MAGIC

FAMILY   Perse (*mother*) | Helios (*father*)
            Pasiphaë (*sister*)
            Aeëtes (*brother*)
            Perses (*brother*) | Ardeas (*son*)
            Latinus (*son*) | Telegonus (*son*)
SYMBOLS   Staff, cup, pig, lion
STRENGTHS   Magic, potions

The sun god Helios married Perse, a child of Oceanus and grandchild of Gaia and Uranus. Helios and Perse had four children, two daughters and two sons.

Their first child was Pasiphaë, who married Minos, the king of Crete, only to fall in love with a bull and give birth to the half-man, half-bull monster known as the Minotaur.

The second was Aeëtes, who became the king of Colchis. Aeëtes owned a golden ram's fleece that his daughter Medea would later help the hero Jason steal.

The third child, Perses, tried to usurp Aeëtes's throne, but Medea killed her uncle and restored her father as king.

Finally, there was Circe: a goddess of magic and one of the most powerful sorceresses the world has ever known. Circe lived on an island called Aeaea. No other gods or mortals lived with her, but she was not alone. Gentle, faded-gold lions roamed all over the sloping fields and crooked cliffs. Speckled wolves with glowing eyes lurked among the trees. At night, the animals slept inside Circe's house, surrounding her bed. Aeaea strained under the weight of its abundance: The trees drooped with fruit, the soil teemed with growth. It offered Circe everything that she needed and integrated everything that she gave it in return.

Circe's house was perched on the highest point of the island. First thing in the morning, she toiled in her garden. After dinner she liked to unwind by weaving on her loom. But her favorite activity—the one that took up most of her day—was magic. She plucked plants she needed for her spells from all over Aeaea. She grew the herbs that she couldn't find. She chopped, she boiled, she stirred. She brewed potions with special powers. She carved a magic staff from the wood of a yew tree. When Circe said the right words or made the right gestures, she could bring about visions, health, love, sleep—even death.

Circe's mind held everything that she learned in a tight grip and didn't let go. Once she mastered a spell or potion, it became instinct. Her greatest talent lay in transformation. She started small: She would turn a fly into a bird or a mouse into a frog, all for her own amusement. After some practice she was able make lions out of her wolves and wolves out of her lions.

On a day like any other, Circe heard someone approach her house, which was a rare event. She went outside to greet the visitor, but stopped in shock at the sight of him. He looked like no one thing that she had seen before, but rather like a mix of things. For the most part, he looked like a man, but his skin and the hair streaming down his back were green flashing blue, as if he had absorbed the colors of the sea. A scaly, flailing fish tail began at his waist. He couldn't be a mortal. Was he a god? Or a monster? Whatever he was, Circe thought, he was enormously pleasing to her eye.

His name, he told her, was Glaucus. He was born a mortal and raised to be a fisherman. He used to spend his days on a boat in the ocean, hauling nets dripping with fish. On his last fishing trip, he happened upon a beach, beside which lay a meadow. He went ashore and arranged his fish on the grass. But as soon as he did, the fish got up and walked back into the sea.

Glaucus couldn't believe what he had seen. But he knew that it had happened. The grass, he realized, must have an otherworldly power. He tore off a few blades and stuffed them in his mouth. Scarcely had he swallowed when he was overcome with the urge to walk into the sea as the fish had. He dove under the waves and swam into the deep, propelled by his new tail, until he reached Oceanus, Circe's grandfather and the god who embodied the ocean. Oceanus gladly welcomed Glaucus to his home.

At first, Glaucus was delighted with his life as a god in Oceanus's halls. He didn't have to catch fish to make a living; he could just watch them float by. He slept in large, glass-walled rooms. Every meal was a feast attended by other gods and goddesses and nymphs. But before long, he wanted more; he wanted a wife. He had someone in mind, too: a pretty sea nymph named Scylla, whose luxurious hair billowed like kelp, whose skin was as smooth as the inside of a shell.

Glaucus pursued Scylla relentlessly. "Dear Scylla," he rhapsodized, "for a long time I wondered why the Fates yanked me from the life I had and tossed me into this one. Now I know—I became a god so that I would have an eternity to spend with you."

Scylla looked at his blue-green skin, his fins, his unbearable sincerity, and began to laugh. Glaucus was hurt and embarrassed. But her indifference was not enough to make him give up. This was how he ended up on Circe's doorstep, asking her to make Scylla love him.

Circe had been listening intently to Glaucus's tale. She was taken with him, this god who had tasted mortality and conquered it.

"You don't need a spell for love," she told him. Glaucus's eyes filled with hope. "That is," Circe hastily added, "because I am willing to love you even if that foolish Scylla is not."

Glaucus was taken aback. "Thank you, Goddess," he replied, "but I will love Scylla, or I will love nobody at all."

Circe felt in turns chill and heat. Who was he to reject her? She was a daughter of Helios. He was a mortal who became a god by chance and a handful of grass. He spent his days groveling to her grandfather. But there was still affection mixed with her contempt. She didn't wish to do him harm. She would punish her rival instead.

She picked a few herbs from her garden and brewed a new potion throughout the night. Circe happened to know that Scylla liked to bathe in this one pool on the side of a strait. When the potion had finished brewing, Circe draped herself in a blue cloak and headed for Scylla's favorite bathing spot.

It was early in the day, so Scylla wasn't there yet. Circe poured the potion into the water and watched the inky tendrils swirl around. Then, she sailed home, giddy with the pleasure of having done a terrible thing.

Not long after Circe departed, Scylla arrived. She undid her robe and settled in the pool. But before she had a chance to relax, the water around her started bubbling. Scylla screamed—she felt as though someone were pulling at her limbs, trying to rip them off. She sprouted six heads with knife-sharp teeth, attached to long necks. Below her waist was a ring of rabid dogs. Her legs splintered into a dozen thrashing tentacles. The once-lovely Scylla was now a terrible monster. She stayed in the strait, her many mouths snatching any sailors who were brave or foolish enough to pass by. A second sea monster, Charybdis, lived under a small rock on the other side of the strait. Passing between the two of them often led sailors to a bloody end.

That wasn't the last time Circe's transformation skills made waves. She thought that she would finally get over Glaucus when she met Picus, the king of Latium, but he rejected her, too, saying that his heart belonged to another. Circe was so mad that, almost before she knew what was happening, she muttered a spell and turned him into a woodpecker. But Circe's most significant act of magic transformed her own life.

Circe was at home, weaving, when she heard a noise outside. She rushed to her window and saw twenty-two men trudging up the hill toward her house. They didn't look like they had come to ask for her magical aid, she noted: Their clothes were tattered, their bodies were heavy with exhaustion, and their faces showed mostly confusion. Even with her potions, staff, and divinity, Circe was worried about being alone with so many men. She wouldn't be able to fight them off, if it came to that. She had to use her mind.

By the time Circe opened the door for the men, she had a plan. She invited them inside. She sat them at her large wooden table. She brought out an assortment of dishes: fish, cheese, bread, fruit. She also poured each man some wine.

Unbeknownst to them, she had mixed into the dark liquid an even darker potion. The men were so happy to see good wine that they drank it in big gulps, barely stopping to breathe. While they were still dazed with satisfaction, Circe whipped out her staff and struck each one on the head.

The transformation started immediately, but lasted long enough for Circe to delight in what she had done. The men started to scream as they felt their bodies fold into themselves, but their screams were choked into squeals. They grew shorter and broader. Each of them sprouted a curl of a tail from the seat of their pants.

Circe had twenty-one new pigs, all plump and a lovely pale pink.

Wait—twenty-one? Circe counted them again. Hadn't she seen twenty-two men from her window? One must have broken away from the group before dinner.

Circe shrugged. The missing man wouldn't be happy when he found out what she had done to his friends. But what could he do? She was an immortal goddess, a powerful sorceress. He was just one man. She thought no more of him and drove the pigs to the back of her house, where she had a pen waiting. She closed the gate and tossed them some scraps, although they were too full and frightened to eat.

She went back inside, prepared to spend the rest of the evening at her loom. But her rest was interrupted by another knock. When she opened the door, another man stood there. Had the twenty-second come back? Another pig for me, she thought as she let him in.

She brought out the leftovers from the first dinner for her guest. And, of course, some wine. She watched, a smile never leaving her face, as he ate and drank. He was more restrained than the others, she noted. He ate his meal slowly. He made polite conversation with Circe, asking her about the island, the lions and wolves, her loom. By the time he finished his last bites of bread and cheese, she was almost sorry for what she was about to do.

Circe reached for her staff, prepared to strike. But as soon as she moved, or maybe a bit before, he moved too. He drew his sword and knocked away her staff, then rested the blade on the tender curve of her neck. Circe was more impressed than scared. She tucked her staff back into her belt.

"The potion didn't work," she said slowly. She thought of an herb called *moly*, the one thing that could have blocked her magic. Another thought came to mind: Only gods could safely harvest moly. This man had had divine help. He was favored by the gods, or at least *one* god. But which? "Where did you get the moly?"

"Hermes," the man admitted. He moved his sword away from her neck.

Of course the trickster god was involved, Circe thought. She could just picture him in his winged sandals, laughing. Suddenly, she remembered Hermes telling her that a man whose mind was like a labyrinth would come to Aeaea one day. "And who are you?"

 80

The man leaned back into his chair and began to talk. His name was Odysseus, he said, and he was the king of Ithaca. About a year ago—maybe less, maybe more—the great war in Troy had ended. After a decade of fighting, he could finally go home to his family. But the Fates had other ideas that even Athena, his protector, couldn't change. First, storms blew his ships to the island of the Lotus-Eaters, who fed his crew lotuses that made them not want to leave. Odysseus had to drag them back to the ships.

That was only the beginning of Odysseus's troubles. Next, he landed on an island with a cave inhabited by the Cyclops Polyphemus, who ate some of the crew. Odysseus and his remaining men eventually escaped by getting Polyphemus drunk and blinding him with a stake. Then they visited the home of Aeolus, who made the west wind help them with their journey and gave Odysseus the other winds in a bag. But while he was asleep, his men opened the bag and the winds blew the ships right back to Aeolus, who refused to help them again.

So they sailed on to the island of the Laestrygonians, man-eating giants who destroyed every ship except Odysseus's. By the time they reached Aeaea, his crew consisted of one ship and a handful of men.

Upon landing, Odysseus sent some of his crew ahead of him to scout for shelter while he waited by the ship. One of the men, Eurylochus, came running back in a panic. He claimed that a witch lived on the island. The rest of the men went into her house, but Eurylochus stayed behind, suspecting treachery. He then watched with horror from the window as she turned the men into pigs. He insisted that they leave with the remaining men straightaway.

But Odysseus wouldn't listen to Eurylochus; he decided to go to the witch's house too. He was almost there when he ran into Hermes, who gave him the moly.

Circe rose from the table. "I will set your men free. All of you may stay here as long as you need. But for now, come to bed with me. Nothing builds trust like sharing a bed."

"First, swear that you will do me no harm," he said. "Swear it by the gods."

"I swear it."

For the next year, Circe and Odysseus lived together in bliss on Aeaea. They feasted and drank wine all day, joined by Odysseus's men, whom Circe had released from the pig hides. At night, they lay in each other's arms and talked. Odysseus told her stories about the war: clashes between heroes like Achilles and Hector, and Olympians like Ares and Athena. But his favorite subject was Penelope, his wife, and Telemachus, his son. Penelope, he said, was the kindest, most faithful woman who had ever lived, not to mention a great weaver. He liked to imagine how Telemachus, who was just an infant when Odysseus left for Troy, had grown up. Talking about them seemed to bring him a complicated kind of joy: He would shine brightly, then fall into a deep melancholy.

Increasingly, Odysseus appeared to take less pleasure in his routines with Circe. Sometimes he sat by himself on a cliff and stared at the sea for hours. Circe tried to jolt him out of his sadness with more good food and wine, music and talk. But he continued to wilt. When spring came and he was still like that, Circe knew that she had to let him go back to his wife and son in Ithaca.

She found him on his usual cliff. "King Odysseus, it is time for you to go home," she said. "But first you must go to the Underworld and find the blind prophet Tiresias. He will tell you what to do."

"The Underworld? Where no man has ever sailed?" Odysseus began to weep, thinking that he was going to his death.

"Do not worry. Just go." Circe gave him directions. The next morning, Odysseus would sail for the home of Hades. Even though Circe knew that Athena was protecting him, she breathed more easily once she saw his ship returning intact to Aeaea.

"Let us now eat and drink our fill," she said to Odysseus and his men. "You sail for Ithaca at dawn."

At the feast, Odysseus was more animated than he had been in months. Circe ate very little, watching his every move. The two of them didn't sleep at all that night. They talked about the voyage to come. Circe warned Odysseus that he would pass the Sirens: half-woman, half-bird creatures with irresistible singing voices. Many a sailor had died while trying to get closer to the Sirens' rocky island. Odysseus would also sail the narrow strait between the two sea monsters Scylla and Charybdis. After a moment's hesitation, she told him the story of how Scylla came to be. If he survived Scylla, he would reach an island where Circe's father, Helios, kept his cows. He must not touch the cows, she said, or his homecoming would take even longer.

When Eos, goddess of the dawn, poked her rosy fingers through the clouds, Circe knew that she could not delay him any further. She walked him to the beach, where the early morning tide was calmly lapping the shore. Odysseus's men stood on their ship, waiting.

Circe dreaded his departure so much that she needed him to leave at once: The looming threat of pain felt worse than the pain ever could. Even as he held both her hands and spoke tender words of farewell, she could tell that already his mind was not with her, but with Siren tunes and sea monsters and sacred cows. Their time together was just another leg of his journey. Their separation was just another hardship to overcome. In time—not even a lot of time—he would overcome it.

Circe watched Odysseus board the ship, watched the ship grow smaller and smaller until the horizon zapped it into nothingness. She knew that he would move on to bigger and more exciting adventures. She knew that she would not hear about them for many years, maybe not until Odysseus had passed into the Underworld. She would never see him again. She thought this with certainty and relief. She did not ever want to learn that the man with whom she had spent every hour of the last year had forgotten her or stopped caring.

As for Circe? She thought that her life would stand still. She would never grow old or die. There would be scant evidence that time had passed at all.

But that isn't what happened. Shortly after Odysseus left, Circe started to feel sick in the mornings, sometimes for the entire day. She spent most of her time horizontal on the grass, her lions occasionally approaching to lick her brow in concern. Soon, her belly developed a soft curve. The following year she bore three sons: Ardeas, Latinus, and Telegonus.

Now Circe's days were full, loud, and absurd. They felt at once too short and too long. Ardeas and Latinus were cheerful, obedient boys, happy with their lives on the island. But Telegonus was different. He was constantly asking questions about the world beyond Aeaea, to which Circe gave vague, evasive answers. He was particularly curious about his father. So it came as no surprise when Telegonus, now a young man, announced that he was sailing to Ithaca to find Odysseus.

Circe did not love the idea of her son undertaking such a long, dangerous voyage. But Telegonus was grown up; he was his own person. Circe could not stop him from leaving. She packed a boat for him and sent him to Ithaca.

After what felt to her like a long time, but was actually shorter than she had expected, Telegonus returned to Aeaea. Circe was surprised to see that he had company: a woman and a man. Telegonus told her, through tears, what had happened.

Telegonus arrived in Ithaca safely but without any supplies left. He had started foraging for food when he heard a shout. Two men were charging toward him. The older one was saying that he was the king of Ithaca and it was his job to protect it from thieves. Telegonus, realizing that the man was his father, tried to explain himself, but Odysseus wouldn't listen. They got into a fight. While trying to defend himself, Telegonus accidentally killed Odysseus with the stingray spine that he carried as a weapon.

Telegonus was numb. He looked to the younger man, who couldn't seem to believe that Odysseus was dead. When their eyes met, Telegonus knew who the boy must be.

When Telegonus finished his tale, Circe realized who the woman and man with him were: Penelope and Telemachus, Odysseus's wife and son. She had heard so many stories about them, and now they were in her house. Her son had brought them to Aeaea so that they could bury Odysseus here. It was what Athena wanted, Telegonus explained.

Circe's past and the future were coming together. Why did Athena send Odysseus back to her? Perhaps she wanted him to be with his entire family in the end. Perhaps she wanted the two sides of his family to be with each other.

They buried Odysseus in the island's loveliest spot. Afterward, Circe brewed one of the most powerful potions she had ever thought up and offered it to Penelope and Telemachus. When they finished the last drop, they looked the same. But inside they were forever changed: changed to live forever, as immortal as Circe herself.

Circe now had more than lions and wolves for company: She had family. Together, they would live out their days on Aeaea, days that would never run out.

MYTHOLOGICAL CREATURES

CERBERUS

The three-headed, snake-tailed dog that guards the gates to the Underworld and stops the dead from escaping.

CENTAURS

Human from the waist up, horse from the waist down. The most famous centaur is Chiron, the teacher of many heroes.

CHARYBDIS

A sea monster that lives opposite **Scylla** and drowns passing sailors by making whirlpools.

CHARON

The ferryman who transports dead souls across the river Styx to Hades. Gold coins were placed over the eyes or under the tongue of the deceased to pay Charon's fare.

CHIMERA

A creature with a lion's head, goat's body, and snake's tail that also breathes fire. The word "chimera" now refers to an unlikely fantasy.

CYCLOPES

One-eyed giants that made weapons such as Zeus's thunderbolt and Poseidon's trident. Poseidon had a Cyclops son, Poly-phemus, who trapped Odysseus after Odys-seus washed up on Polyphemus's island.

ERINYES (FURIES)

Born from the blood of Uranus, the Erinyes are goddesses of revenge who punish mortals for crimes that violate the natural order, such as murdering a family member.

GORGONS

Three sisters with wings and with hair made of venomous snakes. Anyone who looked at them turned into stone. The hero Perseus killed one of the Gorgons, **Medusa**, and gave her head to Athena, who put it on her shield.

GRAEAE

Three sisters in the form of old women named Deino, Enyo, and Pemphredo. They take turns using one eye and one tooth.

HARPIES

Wind spirits with a woman's head and a vulture's body. They steal food and bring victims to the **Erinyes** and the Underworld, torturing them along the way.

HYDRA

A many-headed water monster with venomous breath and blood. For every head you cut off, it would grow back two. Heracles killed it by sealing the wounds with fire.

MINOTAUR

A monster with the head of a bull and the body of a man that King Minos of Crete imprisoned in a labyrinth. The Minotaur fed on sacrificial victims from Athens until the hero Theseus killed it.

NEMEAN LION

A lion whose claws
could cut through
armor and whose fur
protected it from all
weapons. In the end,
the hero Heracles
had to strangle it
with his bare hands.

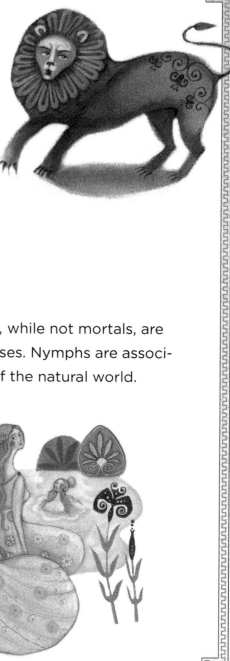

NYMPHS

Beautiful women who, while not mortals, are
also not quite goddesses. Nymphs are associated with the forces of the natural world.

PEGASUS

A winged horse born from the blood of **Medusa** after Perseus cut off her head. The hero Bellerophon rode Pegasus while fighting the **Chimera**.

SATYRS

Creatures with the upper half of a man and the lower half of a goat. Satyrs love to get drunk and party. They were companions of the god Pan, who looked and acted just like them.

SCYLLA

Circe turned Scylla, once a water nymph, into a sea monster out of jealousy. The phrase "between Scylla and **Charybdis**" means having to choose between two bad options.

SIRENS

Creatures with women's heads, birds' bodies, and irresistible voices. Their singing is so enchanting that sailors who hear it sail closer and shipwreck on their rocky island.

SPHINX

A creature with a human head, a lion's body, and wings. It tells riddles, killing and eating those who answer incorrectly.

TYPHON

An immensely strong giant with fire-breathing snakes sprouting from his shoulders. He and his wife Echidna—who had the head of a woman on the body of a snake—had many monstrous children together, including **Cerberus**, the **Hydra**, the **Chimera**, the **Sphinx**, and the **Nemean Lion**.

PRONUNCIATION GUIDE

ACHILLES *(uh-KIL-eez)*: The best of the Greek warriors

ACTAEON *(ak-TEE-uhn)*: A hunter whom Artemis turned into a stag

ADMETUS *(ad-MEE-tuhs)*: King of Thessaly; husband of Alcestis

ADONIS *(uh-DON-is)*: A handsome mortal lover of Aphrodite

AEAEA *(ee-EE-uh)*: Circe's island

AEËTES *(ee-EE-teez)*: King of Colchis; brother of Circe; father of Medea

AENEAS *(ih-NEE-uhs)*: Hero of Troy; ancestor of the Romans

AEOLUS *(EE-uh-luhs)*: Keeper of the winds

AETHER (EE-ther): Personification of the upper air

AGAMEMNON *(ag-uh-MEM-non)*: King of Mycenae; leader of the Greeks during the Trojan War

ALCESTIS *(al-SES-tis)*: Queen of Thessaly; Wife of Admetus

ALCMENE *(alk-MEE-nee)*: Mother of Heracles

ALTHAEA *(al-THEE-uh)*: Queen of Calydon; wife of Oeneus; mother of Meleager

AMALTHEA *(am-uhl-THEE-uh)*: The goat who raised baby Zeus

ANCHISES *(an-KY-seez)*: Prince of Troy; father of Aeneas

APHRODITE *(aah-fro-DIE-tee)*: Goddess of love and beauty

APOLLO *(uh-POL-oh)*: God of the sun

ARACHNE *(uh-RAK-nee)*: A talented mortal weaver

ARDEAS *(ahr-DEE-us)*: Son of Circe and Odysseus

ARES *(AIR-eez)*: God of war

ARETHUSA *(ar-uh-THOO-zuh)*: A nymph who turned into a spring

ARGES *(AHR-jeez)*: A Cyclops

ARGUS PANOPTES *(AHR-guhs pan-OP-teez)*: A giant with eyes all over his body

ARTEMIS *(AHR-tuh-miss)*: Goddess of the moon

ASCALAPHUS *(uh-SKAL-luh-fuhs)*: Gardener of the Underworld

ASCLEPIUS *(uh-SKLEE-pee-uhs)*: God of medicine

ATALANTA *(at-ah-LAN-tuh)*: A huntress who took part in the Calydonian boar hunt

ATHENA *(uh-THEE-nuh)*: Goddess of wisdom and war

ATLAS *(AT-luhs)*: A Titan who supports the world on his shoulders

ATROPOS *(AH-truh-pos)*: The Fate who cuts the thread of life

AUGEAN STABLES *(aw-JEE-uhn)*: The stables of Augeus, the king of Elis, which held three thousand oxen and had not been cleaned in thirty years

BRIAREUS *(brai-AIR-ee-uhs)*: One of the Hecatonchires

BRONTES *(BRON-teez)*: A Cyclops

CALLIOPE *(kuh-LY-uh-pee)*: The Muse of epic poetry

CATTLE OF GERYON *(GE-ree-on)*: The cattle of a winged monster with three bodies

CENTAUR *(SEN-tawr)*: Half-human, half-horse

CERBERUS *(SUR-ber-uhs)*: A dog with three heads that guards the entrance to the Underworld

CERYNEIAN *(keh-ruh-NEE-uhn)* Hind: A female deer with golden antlers, sacred to Artemis, that could outrun an arrow

CETO *(SEE-toh)*: Primordial sea goddess

CHAOS *(KAY-os)*: The void that preceded the universe

CHARON *(KAIR-uhn)*: The ferryman of the Underworld who transports the souls of the dead across the River Styx

CHARYBDIS *(kuh-RIB-dis)*: A sea monster that lives across from Scylla

CHIMERA *(ki-MEER-uh)*: A monster with a lion's head, goat's body, and snake's tail

CIRCE *(SER-see)*: A goddess of magic

CLIO *(KLEE-oh)*: The Muse of history

CLOTHO *(KLOH-thoh)*: The Fate who spins the thread of life

COEUS *(KOY-uhs)*: A Titan

COLCHIS *(KOL-kis)*: A wealthy kingdom in the East

CORONIS *(kuh-ROH-nis)*: Princess of Thessaly; mother of Asclepius

COTTUS *(KAW-tuhs)*: One of the Hecatonchires

CRETAN BULL *(KREE-tuhn)*: The bull that fathered the Minotaur with Pasiphaë, queen of Crete

CRIUS *(KRY-uhs)*: A Titan

CRONUS *(KROH-nuhs)*: A Titan who overthrew his father Uranus to rule the heavens until his son Zeus overthrew him

CYCLOPES *(sai-KLOH-peez)*: One-eyed giants

DEINO *(DAY-noh)*: One of the Graeae

DELOS *(DEE-los)*: The island where Artemis and Apollo were born

DEMETER *(duh-MEE-tur)*: Goddess of the harvest

DIONYSUS *(die-uh-NY-suhs)*: God of wine

ECHIDNA *(ih-KID-nuh)*: A half-woman, half-snake monster

ECHO *(EK-oh)*: A mountain nymph who can only repeat the last words said to her

EILEITHYIA *(il-luh-THY-uh)*: Goddess of midwifery

ENYO *(ih-NY-oh)*: One of the Graeae

EOS *(EE-os)*: Goddess of the dawn

ERATO *(ER-uh-toh)*: The Muse of love poetry

EREBUS *(ER-uh-buhs)*: Personification of darkness

ERINYES *(ih-RIN-ee-eez)*: The Furies, goddesses of vengeance

ERIS *(ER-is)*: Goddess of discord

EROS *(ER-os)*: God of love

ERYMANTHIAN BOAR *(er-uh-MAN-thee-uhn)*: A wild boar that terrorized Arcadia

EUROPA *(yoo-ROH-puh)*: A princess of Phoenicia whom Zeus abducted while in the form of a bull and took to Crete; mother of Minos

EURYBIA *(yoo-RIB-ee-uh)*: A Titan

EURYLOCHUS *(yoo-RIL-luh-kuhs)*: Odysseus's second-in-command

EURYSTHEUS *(yoo-RIS-thee-uhs)*: King of Tiryns, who imposed the Twelve Labors on Heracles

EUTERPE *(yoo-TUR-pee)*: The Muse of music

GAIA *(GUY-ah)*: Goddess of the earth

GLAUCUS *(GLAH-kuhs)*: A mortal fisherman who turned into a sea god after eating a magical herb

GORGONS *(GAWR-guhns)*: Three sisters with wings and with hair made of venomous snakes

GRAEAE *(GRAY-ee)*: Three sisters who take turns using one eye and one tooth

GYGES *(JY-jeez)*: One of the Hecatonchires

HADES *(HAY-deez)*: God of the Underworld

HARPIES *(HAHR-peez)*: Wind spirits with women's heads and vultures' bodies

HEBE *(HEE-bee)*: The Olympian cupbearer

HECATONCHIRES *(heck-uh-tawn-KEHR-rehz)*: Giants with fifty heads and a hundred arms

HECTOR *(HECK-tur)*: The eldest prince and greatest warrior of Troy

HELEN *(HEL-uhn)*: Queen of Sparta; the most beautiful woman in the world

HELIOS *(HEE-lee-ohs)*: God of the sun

HEMERA *(HEH-meh-ruh)*: Personification of day

HEPHAESTUS *(hih-FES-tuhs)*: The blacksmith god

HERA *(HEH-rah)*: Goddess of women, marriage, childbirth, and family; queen of the gods

HERACLES *(HEH-ruh-kleez)*: The greatest of the Greek heroes

HERMES *(HER-meez)*: The messenger god

HESPERIDES *(heh-SPER-uh-deez)*: Nymphs of the evening

HESTIA *(HES-tee-uh)*: Goddess of the hearth

HIPPOCRENE *(HIP-uh-kreen)*: A spring sacred to the Muses

HIPPOLYTA *(hih-POL-ih-tuh)*: Queen of the Amazons

HYDRA *(HY-druh)*: A many-headed water monster with venomous breath and blood

HYPERION *(hy-PEER-ee-uhn)*: A Titan

IAPETUS *(eye-AP-uh-tuhs)*: A Titan

IO *(EYE-oh)*: Princess of Argos

ITHACA *(ITH-uh-kuh)*: An Ionian island; the home of Odysseus

JASON *(JAY-suhn)*: A Greek hero and leader of the Argonauts

JUNO *(JOO-noh)*: The Roman name for Hera

KOURETES *(koo-RAY-teez)*: Followers of Rhea

LACHESIS *(LACH-uh-sis)*: The Fate who measures the thread
of life

LAESTRYGONIANS *(les-trih-GOH-nee-uhnz)*: Man-
eating giants

LATINUS *(luh-TY-nuhs)*: Son of Circe and Odysseus

LATIUM *(LAY-shee-um)*: An ancient Italian city that later
became the site of Rome

LETO *(LEE-toh)*: Mother of Artemis and Apollo

MARES OF DIOMEDES *(die-uh-MEE-deez)*: A herd of
man-eating horses

MEDEA *(mih-DEE-uh)*: Princess of Colchis; sorceress

MEDUSA *(muh-DOO-suh)*: A Gorgon whose gaze turned people
into stone

MELEAGER *(mel-lee-AY-gur)*: Prince of Calydon and a
Greek hero

MELIAE *(MEE-lee-ee)*: Nymphs of the ash tree

MELPOMENE *(mel-POM-uh-nee)*: The Muse of tragedy

MENELAUS *(men-uh-LAY-uhs)*: King of Sparta; husband
of Helen

METIS *(MEE-tis)*: A Titaness; mother of Athena

MINOS *(MY-nuhs)*: King of Crete

MINOTAUR *(MIN-uh-tawr)*: A monster with the head of a bull
and the body of a man

MNEMOSYNE *(nee-MOS-uh-nee)*: A Titaness; goddess
of memory

MOIRAI *(MOY-rye)*: Another name for the Fates

MOUNT HELICON *(HEL-ih-kawn)*: Home of the Muses

MUSES *(MYOO-zuhz)*: Goddesses of inspiration

MYCENAE *(my-SEE-nee)*: An ancient Greek city

NARCISSUS *(nahr-SIS-uhs)*: A handsome youth who fell in love with his own reflection

NEREUS *(NEER-ee-uhs)*: A sea god

NIOBE *(ny-OH-bee)*: Queen of Thebes

NYMPHS *(nimfz)*: Female spirits associated with forces of the natural world

NYX *(niks)*: Personification of the night

OCEANUS *(oh-SEE-uh-nuhs)*: God who embodies the ocean

ODYSSEUS *(oh-DIS-ee-uhs)*: King of Ithaca; a hero of the Trojan War, after which he took a ten-year journey back home

OENEUS *(EE-nee-uhs)*: King of Calydon; husband of Althaea; father of Meleager

OUREA *(ooh-REE-ah)*: Primordial gods of the mountains

PAPHOS *(PAY-fos)*: The place where Aphrodite rose from the sea

PARIS *(PAR-is)*: Prince of Troy; eloped with Helen, causing the Trojan War

PASIPHAË *(puh-SIF-ee)*: Queen of Crete; wife of Minos; mother of the Minotaur

PEGASUS *(PEG-uh-suhs)*: A winged horse

PELEUS *(PEE-lee-uhs)*: King of Pythia; husband of Thetis; father of Achilles

PEMPHREDO *(pem-FREE-doh)*: One of the Graeae

PENELOPE *(puh-NEL-uh-pee)*: Queen of Ithaca; wife of Odysseus; mother of Telemachus; remained faithful to her absent husband for twenty years

PERSE *(PUR-see)*: An Oceanid nymph; wife of Helios; mother of Circe

PERSEPHONE *(pur-SEF-uh-nee)*: Queen of the Underworld; daughter of Demeter and Zeus

PERSES *(PUR-seez)*: Brother of Circe and Aeëtes; usurped Aeëtes's throne but was then murdered by Medea

PHERAE *(FEER-ee)*: A city in Thessaly

PHOEBE *(FEE-bee)*: A Titaness

PHORCYS *(FAWR-sis)*: A sea god

PICUS *(PY-kuhs)*: King of Latium

PIERIDES *(py-AIR-uh-deez)*: The nine daughters of Pierus who challenged the Muses to a singing contest

PIERUS *(PY-ruhs)*: King of Emathia; father of the Pierides

POLYHYMNIA *(pol-ih-HIM-nee-uh)*: The Muse of hymns

POLYPHEMUS *(pol-ih-FEE-muhs)*: A Cyclops who eats Odysseus's men

PONTUS *(PON-tuhs)*: Personification of the sea

POSEIDON *(poh-SY-duhn)*: God of the sea

PYRENEUS *(py-REE-nee-uhs)*: King of Thrace; tried to trap the Muses in his palace

RHEA *(RAY-ah):* A Titaness; mother of the Olympian gods and goddesses

RIVER STYX *(stiks)*: A river in the Underworld

SATYRS *(SAY-turs)*: Half-man, half-goat creatures that love to drink and party

SCYLLA *(SIL-uh)*: A sea monster that lives across from Charybdis

SIRENS *(SY-ruhns)*: Half-woman, half-bird creatures with enchanting singing voices

SPHINX *(sfinks)*: A creature with a human head, lion's body, and wings, that tells riddles and eats those who can't answer

STEROPES *(stuh-ROH-peez)*: A Cyclops

STYMPHALIAN BIRDS *(stim-FAY-lee-uhn)*: Man-eating birds with bronze beaks and metallic feathers

TARTARUS *(TAHR-ter-uhs)*: The dungeons deep below the Underworld

TELEGONUS *(tuh-LEG-uh-nuhs)*: Son of Circe and Odysseus

TELEMACHUS *(tuh-LEM-uh-kuhs)*: Prince of Ithaca; son of Odysseus and Penelope

TERPSICHORE *(turp-SIK-uh-ree)*: The Muse of dance

TETHYS *(TEE-this)*: A Titaness; wife of Oceanus

THALIA *(THEY-lee-uh)*: The Muse of comedy

THAUMAS *(THAH-muhs)*: A sea god

THEBES *(theebz)*: An ancient Greek city

THEIA *(THEE-uh)*: A Titaness

THEMIS *(THEE-mis)*: A Titaness

THETIS *(THEE-tis)*: A sea nymph; wife of Peleus; mother of Achilles

TIRESIAS *(ty-REE-see-uhs)*: A blind prophet

TIRYNS *(TIR-inz)*: An ancient Greek city

TITANS *(TY-tuhns)*: Pre-Olympian gods

TYPHON *(TY-fon)*: A giant monster with a hundred fire-breathing snakes on his shoulders

URANIA *(yoo-RAY-nee-uh)*: The Muse of astronomy

URANUS *(yoo-RAY-nus)*: Personification of the heavens and ruler of the universe until his son Cronus overthrew him

ZEUS *(zoos)*: God of thunder; king of the gods

RESOURCES

ANCIENT TEXTS

Ovid (trans. David Raeburn), *Metamorphoses*

Hesiod (trans. Stanley Lombardo), *Theogony*

Homer (trans. Robert Fagles), *Iliad*

Homer (trans. Emily Wilson), *The Odyssey*

Pseudo-Apollodorus (trans. Robin Hard), *The Library of Greek Mythology*

Virgil (trans. Robert Fagles), *The Aeneid*

CHILDREN'S BOOKS

Ingri and Edgar Parin d'Aulaire, *D'Aulaires' Book of Greek Myths*

Joan Holub and Suzanne Williams, *Goddess Girls* (series)

Kate McMullan, *Myth-O-Mania* (series)

Donna Jo Napoli, *Treasury of Greek Mythology: Classic Stories of Gods, Goddesses, Heroes & Monsters*

George O'Connor, *Olympians* (series)

Rick Riordan, *Percy Jackson and the Olympians* (series)

Rick Riordan, *Percy Jackson's Greek Gods*

Ann Turnbull, *Greek Myths*

ADVANCED READERS

Stephen Fry, *Mythos*

Edith Hamilton, *Mythology: Timeless Tales of Gods and Heroes*

Emily Hauser, *For the Most Beautiful: A Novel of the Women of Troy*

Ursula K. Le Guin, *Lavinia*

Madeline Miller, *Circe*

John Spurling, *Arcadian Nights: The Greek Myths Reimagined*

ACKNOWLEDGMENTS

I was able to write this book thanks to my Classics professors at Princeton and Cambridge. It was there that I gained the knowledge that I share in these pages, the training to communicate what I know effectively, and an understanding of why all of this is important.

I would also like to acknowledge my editorial team for their support and guidance throughout the process, in particular Joe Cho and Mary Colgan. Joe was the one who first floated the idea of me writing this book and fought to make it happen every step of the way. Mary looked at and critiqued each word that I turned in; the book is undoubtedly better because of her help.

Finally, I'm grateful for the encouragement from my family and friends, especially my *Eidolon* co-editors, my best friends: Donna Zuckerberg, Sarah Scullin, and Tori Lee. This is for them and their children.

ABOUT THE AUTHOR

Yung In Chae is a writer and Editor-at-Large of *Eidolon*, an online magazine dedicated to the classics. She has an A.B. in Classics from Princeton University and an MPhil in Classics from the University of Cambridge, where she was a Gates Cambridge Scholar. Her writing has appeared in the *New York Times*, the *Times Literary Supplement*, and more. She is from Seoul, South Korea.

yunginchae.com
Twitter: @yunginchae